UNICORN
FOOD

UNICORN
FOOD

Beautiful Plant-Based Recipes
to Nurture Your Inner Magical Beast

KAT ODELL

Workman Publishing · New York

Library of Congress Cataloging-in-Publication Data is available.

ISBN 978-1-5235-0213-4

Design by Becky Terhune
Photography by AJ Meeker
Food styling by Rebecca Jurkevich
Prop styling by Kaitlyn Du Ross Walker
Illustrations by Michelle Mildenberg
Author portrait by Nicole Franzen
Additional photos: *Adobe Stock:* vi-vii, 3, 4 (background and inset), 24 (background),
30–31, 49, 53, 59, 76, 92–93, 106–107, 110–111, 112–113, 118, 160, 164–165, 169.
Getty Images: Iri_sha/iStock 108–109; Larry Landolfi/Science Source viii.
Shutterstock.com: FooTToo 50 (background) and Olena Ukhova 50 (inset);
Vladislav T. Jirousek 154 (background); Zakharchuk 114 (background).

Workman books are available at special discounts when purchased in bulk for premiums
and sales promotions as well as for fund-raising or educational use. Special editions or book
excerpts can also be created to specification. For details, contact the Special Sales Director
at the address below, or send an email to specialmarkets@workman.com.

Workman Publishing Co., Inc.
225 Varick Street
New York, NY 10014-4381

workman.com

WORKMAN is a registered trademark of Workman Publishing Co., Inc.

Printed in China
First printing July 2018

10 9 8 7 6 5 4 3 2 1

To my family—

Mom, Dad, Peter, Olive, and Tiger.

Mom and Dad—

Thank you for always making
me try everything once.

Contents

From medicinal mushrooms and Chinese herbs to gluten-free flours and healthy sweeteners and fats, here you'll find all the essential info on the basics used to build a unicorn pantry. While some ingredients may sound unusual, they're all actually very simple to source.

This chapter is dedicated to simple, delicious nut milks and other beverages that use these alternative milks and other healthful liquids as their base. From hot to cold, sweet to savory, these good-for-you refreshments are a great start to any morning or can be consumed as an afternoon snack. Think of this chapter as a jumping-off point—many of the foods that come later in this book incorporate these delicately flavored, wholesome milks.

Why not eat brunch foods all day, every day? Especially when these dishes are inspired by Australian café culture, where healthy sweet and savory dishes—from Hazelnut-Mocha Overnight Oats (page 57) to Sweet + Sour Rainbow Radish Tacos (page 88)—are enjoyed from a.m. to p.m.

Bonus Mini-Chapter!

Let's Get Wasted It can be challenging to avoid food waste—an issue faced by many home cooks. In my own kitchen, I try to cook with all parts of any given ingredient, like repurposing the almond pulp left over from making almond milk, and finding a way to make palatable those tough stems you remove when cooking with kale. This chapter showcases a few ideas for deliciously reusing these traditionally discarded ingredients.

Snacks + Sweets

For those times when you feel a little peckish or crave a treat, the recipes in this chapter include sweet things and "snacky" things that you can eat without feeling guilty. For desserts that means adding sweeteners like fruit, honey, maple syrup, and coconut palm sugar, and for snacks that means using healthy, naturally satisfying ingredients like veggies, whole grains, and seeds as a base.

Slathers, Spreads + Sidekicks

The beauty of condiments is that they can easily elevate simple dishes. Make a few in advance, like the Black Honey Tahini (page 160), which is amazing on chia pudding (see page 56) or as a dip for dried fruit, or the Pastrami Spice (page 173), which gives a savory meatiness to roasted veggies and avocado toast. Keep them on hand for a quick flavor boost!

WHAT IS UNICORN FOOD?

am not great at yoga, I don't own a dehydrator, and I've never been to Burning Man. I moved from New York City to Los Angeles after college, calling myself an Angeleno for close to eight years before returning to my home city for work. Truth of the matter is, I deeply miss the West Coast and the sunny, relaxed LA lifestyle. So, I decided to bring what I could back to New York.

One of the greatest parts about living in Los Angeles was the access to fresh ingredients, whether sourced from any one of the city's ubiquitous farmers' markets or from the healthy market Erewhon. Suffice it to say, it was easy to be lazy and still eat a super-healthy diet while living in Los Angeles. But then I moved to New York . . . and all that changed. No more fresh duck eggs, no more strawberries in December, and worst of all—no more handmade almond milk. That's when I decided to make my own.

I first experimented with homemade almond milk on a whim while living back in LA. I don't have any medical dietary restrictions that would prevent me from drinking dairy milk, rather, I just prefer the taste of a vanilla bean-enhanced, rich glass of almond milk. And after having one too many highly addicting almond milk-based smoothies at my local wellness eatery, Café Gratitude in Venice Beach, I decided to figure out how to make my own. What I quickly found was that homemade almond milk is not just incredibly simple to make, but it outshines anything you'll find at a restaurant or in a refrigerator case. And likewise I found that the occasional bloating I experienced after drinking cow's milk never happened when I subbed in a nut-based alternative.

Since my move back to New York, I've been re-creating Southern California in my kitchen by making a range of alt-milks (almond, cashew, pine nut, coconut, hazelnut, pistachio to name a few) in various hues, colored with natural, health-boosting ingredients such as spirulina (seaweed), matcha (antioxidant-rich green tea powder), turmeric, and more. I got so swept up in milk mania that I decided to start a nut milk business, and after partnering with a friend to host a pop-up at her restaurant, Mimi Cheng's in New York's East Village, I realized I had to name my product. One day, I looked at the rainbow of milks I had created: pink, purple, yellow, orange, blue, green. The milks were colored with ingredients straight from nature, and likewise fortified with myriad good-for-you properties. *It's like nature's magic*, I thought. I started thinking about fun, colorful, somewhat *magical* things, and the word *unicorn* came to mind. And that's when it hit me: My healthy rainbow of milks should be called *Unicorn Milk*.

FROM UNICORN MILK TO UNICORN FOOD

Unicorn Milk has since morphed into Unicorn Food—where I use many of my milks as ingredients to build an array of foods both sweet and savory. But I should backtrack for a moment. In 2014, I decided to change the way I eat. I didn't want to follow a diet per se, but instead listen to my body about the foods that made me feel good and those that made me feel bad. I eliminated most gluten from my diet (I am not totally gluten-free by any means—if there's a slice of Paulie Gee's pizza on the table, I'll likely eat it), deciding not to cook with it or keep gluten-containing ingredients at home. Likewise, I cut down on white refined sugar. There's zero nutritional value in that

Almost Vegan

The foods I eat at home—and the recipes in this book—are almost vegan. That is, they're heavy on the veggies and exclude all animal products with the exception of honey and bee pollen. Although most traditional vegans eschew those ingredients (since they are insect-made), as someone who eats vegan-ish primarily for the health benefits, I have no problem with them; they're filled with antioxidants and other healthful compounds. If you would rather avoid them, you can almost always swap them out for the sweetener of your choice.

stuff, and study after study pegs sugar as our mortal enemy, linking it to numerous diseases. Ditching sugar was a tough one because I have a major sweet tooth, so instead of eliminating it entirely, I switched over to natural, more nutrient-dense sweeteners with a lower glycemic index like coconut palm sugar, raw honey, dates, and maple syrup. This is also how I became an accidental almost-vegan. What I mean by that is, my job requires being an omnivore; when dining at a restaurant, I will try anything on the menu. But at home, I eat a primarily vegan diet (though I do enjoy honey and bee pollen). I didn't set out to do this. It really was an accident. One day I realized that I mostly ate vegetables, fruit, nuts, and seeds and used coconut butter as a cooking fat. I don't buy products marketed to vegans (so much of what's out there is overprocessed), I just eat a vegetable-heavy diet and skip the dairy. And that's how Unicorn Milk led me to Unicorn Food!

The idea behind Unicorn Food is simple: beautiful, delicious, nutritious, and fun foods (and drinks) for the average human looking to slant his/her diet a bit more toward wellness. It focuses on healthy ingredients with vivid, naturally derived colors, and recipes that taste incredible and look gorgeous on the plate. The recipes are easy to make and deceptively healthy. After all, I shouldn't have to tell you that you're eating a gluten-free, vegan muffin—it should be as delicious as any other muffin, except the one I am feeding you is ten times better because it *is* gluten-free, plant based, and made from whole foods. I want to stress that by and large these are approachable recipes that don't require any crazy kitchen equipment—hey, if I can make these in my tiny New York City kitchen, so can you! In fact, many of these recipes are so simple that they don't even involve cooking. Anyone can mix chia seeds and almond milk, I promise you!

One

UNICORN PANTRY

A Guide to Magical Ingredients, Straight from Nature

Straight up, I'll tell you that there are some unusual ingredients—like algae and chia—used throughout this book. From medicinal mushrooms to protein-rich seeds, the way I build my pantry at home is based around nourishing ingredients free of gluten and refined sugar. The great thing, though, is you don't necessarily *need* all these wacky ingredients to make the recipes in the book, and oftentimes you can leave certain ingredients out—the ones that you're adding more for health benefits or a pop of color than for flavor—and still pull off the recipes. You'll notice a Make It Magical box accompanying certain recipes. Those sections offer suggestions on extra nutrition-boosting ingredients that you can add to a given recipe, but that aren't vital for the dish to succeed. While some of these ingredients might sound unfamiliar, for the most part you can find them at a local health food store; many are also available at national chains such as Whole Foods, Publix, and Trader Joe's, or online. Pretty much every single item is just a mouse click away.

I've divided this chapter into sections by ingredient(s) to explain what each one is and how to cook with it at home, outside of the recipes offered here. You'll find everything from nuts and seeds to algae and alt-sugars, from gluten-free grains to a section on making your own natural-dyed sprinkles. When purchasing the following ingredients, you want to buy from reputable sources. I've offered my favorite brands for each ingredient or group of ingredients to eliminate some of the guesswork. Read on to build your own Unicorn Pantry!

On "Superfoods"

You'll notice that the term doesn't exist in this book, other than in this paragraph. I hate that word. Everything these days is called a "superfood." For me that term—which people attribute to ingredients that are especially nutrient rich—has lost its meaning, and so rather than describe an ingredient as a "superfood," I'd rather tell you *why* it's good for you.

Algae

You're probably thinking, *What, you want me to eat algae? That green stuff from the ocean?* Well, yes! Certain algae—such as Blue Majik and spirulina—contain high levels of wellness-promoting antioxidants, vitamins, minerals, and proteins.

SPIRULINA: This protein-rich, blue-green algae, commonly sold as a powder, is frequently added to smoothies thanks to its host of vitamins, minerals, and acids. While scientists continue to study this freshwater plant, it's currently lauded for its myriad health benefits, including lowering blood sugar, helping the body detox from heavy metals, and boosting energy. Spirulina is also a great lung support for anyone suffering from asthma or living in a polluted city, and, in terms of hormonal health, studies have shown that spirulina helps women during premenopause, reducing depression and mood swings.

I like to add spirulina to smoothies, chia pudding, and overnight oats—staining them a dark green color—and the supplement is also great in more savory dishes, sprinkled over a salad or mixed into a dressing. Though spirulina channels an ocean-y seaweed flavor, in general you don't need to add much of it—in some cases, just ⅛ teaspoon—so it doesn't really add much in the way of extra flavor.

My favorite spirulina brand is E3Live.

BLUE MAJIK: While spirulina has been floating around health food circles for some time now, recently a new algae player has appeared: Blue Majik. Also commonly sold in powder form, Blue Majik is made from an extract of spirulina. While spirulina gives white foods a dark green color, Blue Majik, as its name suggests, turns them bright blue. That blue pigment comes from C-Phycocyanin, a powerful antioxidant that helps combat free radicals in the body. It's also a great anti-inflammatory. Sea algae have been used medicinally for a long time, but it's only recently that they've become increasingly popular in foods and beverages. Scientists are still researching how C-Phycocyanin works.

Blue Majik is sold by E3Live.

Bee Pollen

I can't get enough of bee pollen and its honey-sweet flavor! I take a spoonful before working out as an energy booster, and I sprinkle it atop anything and everything from chia pudding to dates dipped in almond butter.

Bee pollen is a vitamin-, mineral-, and protein-rich supplement made from the pollen that bees pick up as they fly from flower to flower. Because of its high nutrient value, it's a great food for added energy. It's also loaded with protein, making it a complete food and one that's easily absorbed. Bee pollen has been used to treat allergies by reducing the histamine reaction in the body and to regenerate skin cells (which is great for skin irritations and inflammation), and it's an effective digestive aid because it also contains helpful enzymes. Just a tablespoon a day can reap many benefits.

My favorite bee pollen brand is Moon Juice.

Cacao

Cacao is the pure, unprocessed form of chocolate before sugar is added. Cacao seeds, called "beans," are harvested from pods. The pods are cracked open and the seeds within are removed, and this is where chocolate begins. Before the beans are processed and sugar is added, cacao has a bitter chocolate flavor. You'll find cacao in various forms, such as nibs (which are cracked beans) and as cacao powder, which is made by cold-pressing unroasted beans. Through the pressing process, cacao butter is separated and just the powder is left. You'll often see "raw" cacao products at health food stores. Since heat kills some of the healthful enzymes in cacao, raw cacao is better for you because those enzymes are kept alive. In general, cacao is considered nutritious because it's high in antioxidants, and some people believe it can lower blood pressure and boost your mood. Cacao is also a nourishing skin food and a gem for women's health. It's high in vitamin C, making it great for antiaging and skin brightening. Because of cacao's nutrient value, adding the powder to a smoothie or baking with it can help curb PMS cravings in a healthy and nutritious way.

My favorite cacao powder brand is Moon Juice.

Chia Seeds

Chia seeds are small, nutrient-rich, edible seeds that expand and form a gel when mixed with a liquid. They are a great source of energy, are considered a complete protein, and contain fiber and essential fatty acids, plus vitamins and minerals. Chia seeds also help line the stomach, making them a strong healing and digestive aid. As a beauty food, chia seeds help nourish your hair, skin, and nails from the inside out. The seeds don't have much flavor on their own, but are often used to form chia puddings (where they add bulk and texture and allow other flavors to shine) and sprinkled atop breakfast bowls for an extra health boost. Chia seeds are also commonly used in baking as an egg replacement since they help to bind ingredients together (see page 12).

I like the chia seeds sold by Navitas Organics.

Chlorophyll

As you probably learned back in school, chlorophyll is the molecule that makes plants green and turns sunlight into energy. In humans, this grassy green supplement, often sold in liquid form, helps the body detox from heavy metals and is also believed to assist in weight loss. Chlorophyll helps alkalize our body and boost immunity and energy. It is loaded with magnesium, which helps balance hormones. Personally, I've found that chlorophyll helps alleviate hangover symptoms. And if you are a frequent traveler you can mix a few drops in water before you fly to help reduce the effects of in-flight radiation and pollution when flying.

My go-to brand for chlorophyll is De Souza's.

Coconut

Over the last few years, coconut has trended as a versatile wellness ingredient touted for its wealth of nutrients, and its heart-healthy fats. One can drink coconut water or milk, eat the fruit's flesh both dry and fresh, and use coconut oil and coconut butter in cooking. Thanks to its moistening nature, coconut oil is also ubiquitous in beauty products, added to lotions, conditioners, and more.

Fresh coconut can be either young or mature. Young coconuts, usually from Asia, have a green or white husk (white if the green has been stripped off). Mature coconuts have that familiar brown hard outer shell and contain less water and a firmer interior flesh, whereas young coconut flesh is soft and gel-like.

COCONUT BUTTER: Coconut butter is the paste that's made from ground coconut flesh. It can be hard or soft depending on the ambient temperature, and it has a sweet, powerfully coconut flavor. It should not be substituted for coconut oil—the two are entirely different products. Coconut butter is more of a spread as opposed to an oil, and you can eat it with a spoon straight from the jar! I add it to smoothies, coffee, baked goods, and plant-based ice cream for richness.

While coconut oil is increasingly available at supermarkets, you can buy coconut butter at health food stores and online at Amazon .com.

COCONUT MILK AND CREAM: Coconut milk is made from blending shredded coconut with hot water and straining the mixture through cheesecloth. The remaining liquid, which is about as thick as whole cow's milk, is coconut milk. (It can be reduced even further to make a great condensed coconut milk condiment, page 168.) While you can make your own coconut milk at home, I opt for the canned variety because it's affordable and widely available at most markets.

After opening a can of coconut milk, you'll notice a thick layer of cream that forms atop (that is, provided you don't shake the can before opening it!). This is known as coconut cream, and it's silky, rich, and luscious because it contains less water than coconut milk and is higher in fat.

When deciding whether to cook with coconut milk or coconut cream, I consider my recipe. If I am looking to add hydration, then I typically reach for coconut milk. But if I am looking to add richness and less liquid, then coconut cream is my move. And, as coconut cream is more concentrated, it's a great choice for making dairy-free ice cream! When buying canned coconut milk, the options you'll usually find are organic and conventional full-fat coconut milk (sometimes labeled as "classic"), "light" coconut milk, and coconut cream. The products sometimes include stabilizers like guar gum, as well. I tend to select pure canned coconut minus any additives, which are often sold at natural foods supermarkes like Whole Foods.

COCONUT NECTAR: This low-glycemic sweetener, rich in minerals and amino acids, plus vitamin C, is made from tapping the blossoms of the coconut palm tree. Thick and syrupy, this caramel-colored sweetener is reminiscent of molasses in terms of taste. I like to add it to drinks since it easily blends in, and to chia pudding as well.

COCONUT OIL: Coconut oil is the oil extracted from a coconut, and it comes either refined (from fresh coconuts) or unrefined (from dried coconuts). While unrefined or "virgin" coconut oil boasts a sweet, nutty coconut taste and aroma, most refined coconut oil is devoid of scent and flavor. Depending on the temperature, coconut oil can either be a liquid, semisolid, or solid. (To solidify coconut oil, just place it in the fridge; to melt it, simply heat it in a pan over low heat—or if your kitchen is like mine, leave it out on the counter.) While both types of coconut oils can be used interchangeably, some people prefer to cook with refined coconut oil since it has a neutral flavor and higher smoke point than unrefined. I typically use unrefined coconut oil when baking sweet dishes, and I use refined coconut oil for savory preps when I don't want to add a coconut flavor. Coconut oil is rich in fatty acids, and contains lauric acid, which is antibacterial, antifungal, and anti-inflammatory.

COCONUT PALM SUGAR: Caramel-coconut-flavored coconut palm sugar is made from coconut nectar that has been boiled and dehydrated. While it contains the same number of calories as white cane sugar, it scores lower on the glycemic index. It also contains minerals such as iron and zinc. And while I do such as the flavor of coconut palm sugar, I tend to use it most in baking because it's granulated, like regular sugar, but contains more minerals and has a pleasant flavor.

COCONUT WATER: Coconut water, with its sweet, nutty taste, is the liquid that naturally forms within coconuts. It's high in electrolytes such as potassium and magnesium, and is especially hydrating. I love drinking fresh coconut water (especially when feeling dehydrated), and I sometimes use it as a base to make iced coffee. While I prefer fresh coconut water straight from the fruit, the one store brand I sometimes buy is Harmless Harvest. It's the only bottled coconut water I've found that tastes fresh.

FLAKED COCONUT: Coconut flakes, which come sweetened or unsweetened and toasted or untoasted, are exactly as they sound—dried flakes of coconut meat. Coconut flakes come in a variety of sizes from small to large. Grated coconut is usually the smallest, followed by shredded coconut, and, finally, flaked coconut. I often use coconut flakes as a garnish on chia pudding, ice cream, cereal, almond-butter toast, and to make colorful natural sprinkles (see page 23).

Gluten-Free Grains and Seeds

AMARANTH: Though many believe amaranth to be a grain, this popular health food is, in fact, a tiny, cream-colored, gluten-free seed. It was first cultivated by the Aztecs 6,000 to 8,000 years ago, and today it's gaining popularity thanks to its high protein and fiber content, in addition to its richness in manganese and magnesium. Amaranth is commonly cooked and served like rice, and it's also used in baked goods.

I like the amaranth sold by Bob's Red Mill.

BROWN RICE FLOUR: Brown rice flour is a nutty-tasting, gluten-free flour made from brown rice. It is more nutritious than white rice flour because the grain's bran, where much of its healthy goodness lies, is left intact. Brown rice flour is high in fiber, magnesium, and vitamin B_6.

The flour is commonly incorporated into gluten-free flour mixes, but on its own it can give baked goods a gritty texture. That's why many blends mix rice flour with other grain flours and starches, such as sorghum flour and potato starch. You can make your own brown rice flour at home simply by buzzing uncooked brown rice in a food processor until it turns into a fine powder. (It will keep, in an airtight container at room temperature, for about a year.)

I like the brown rice flour made by Bob's Red Mill.

BUCKWHEAT: Popular to contrary belief, buckwheat is a gluten-free seed, not an actual grain or wheat! Most commonly found in soba noodles, buckwheat groats—the name for the seeds—have a unique grassy flavor and are commonly sold in health food stores. Buckwheat contains protein, fiber, vitamins, and minerals and is believed to improve digestion and lower cholesterol.

I love to add buckwheat flour to baked foods for extra nutrition, and whole groats serve as a great breakfast cereal when mixed into granola. They also add a pleasing crunch when toasted and added atop both sweet and savory dishes.

FLAXSEED: Flax is a plant whose light brown, nutty-tasting seed can be consumed whole, ground, or pressed into an oil. Flaxseed is revered by the wellness community for its richness in omega-3 and omega-6 fatty acids (the good fats), in addition to fiber and powerful antioxidants known as lignans. Flax can strengthen hair and nails, and it's also great for digestive support, boosting immunity, and acting as an anti-inflammatory. Some research shows that flax can protect against certain types of cancers.

As with chia (see page 8) and psyllium (see below), when you mix flaxseeds with water, a gel forms, and therefore flax also works well as a binding agent in place of eggs in various foods (see page 12). I use flaxseed meal as a binder in cooking, but I also like to add ground or whole flax to smoothies, and sprinkle either atop breakfast bowls and cereal.

I like the whole flaxseeds and the flaxseed meal sold by Bob's Red Mill.

GLUTEN-FREE ALL-PURPOSE FLOUR: Gluten-free all-purpose flour is a product that's made to replace traditional flour in various recipes. To mimic the makeup of wheat as closely as possible, gluten-free all-purpose flour is made from a varying assortment of grains, starches, and other ingredients such as chickpea flour and cornmeal. One of the best gluten-free flours I've come across is made by Zoe Nathan of Huckleberry Cafe in Los Angeles, and in the *Huckleberry* cookbook, she shares her recipe. If you're looking to buy a premade mix from the market, just make sure to read all of the ingredients and make sure there's nothing artificial in the flour.

My favorite is the Gluten-Free All-Purpose Baking Flour made by Bob's Red Mill.

MILLET: Just like amaranth and quinoa, millet is a gluten-free seed that's often categorized as a whole grain. This small, pale yellow ingredient is high in protein and contains calcium and potassium, among other minerals. Millet is often cooked and served like rice, and it has a subtle nutty flavor.

I like the whole-grain millet sold by Bob's Red Mill.

OATS: Oats are a fiber- and mineral-rich cereal grain that can be gluten-free—or not. If you are avoiding gluten, be sure to check the packaging: If the oats are gluten-free, usually the package will say so. Oats are often touted as a health food because they're believed to lower cholesterol. They're also great for digestive support. In most of my recipes, I cook with old-fashioned rolled oats, and also oat flour. You can make oat flour at home by blending oats in a food processor until they turn into a fine powder. Store this powder in an airtight container as you would typical flour; it should stay fresh for about 6 months.

My favorite gluten-free oat brand is Bob's Red Mill.

PSYLLIUM HUSKS: High in fiber, psyllium husks are—you guessed it—the husks of the psyllium plant's seeds. Typically you'll find psyllium husks sold in capsules and as a loose powder. Medically, psyllium is taken for its laxative effects, but because psyllium husks form a gel when mixed with water (like chia and flaxseed, above, or see page 12), they're a useful egg replacer in baked goods (see Medicine Bread, page 125), where they act as a binder. When taken in small doses, psyllium can assist in detoxing the body by cleaning out the gut.

I like to use the psyllium husk powder made by Yerba Prima.

QUINOA (RED AND WHITE): Quinoa (part of the amaranth family), which can come in an array of colors from white to black to red, is an ancient seed that's long been cultivated by the Incas in Peru. Quinoa is lauded as a health food because it contains more protein than any other grain or seed, and it's also high in fiber, calcium, and B vitamins, among other nutrients. Naturally gluten-free, quinoa has a subtle nutty flavor and can be prepared like rice.

TEFF: Teff is a gluten-free, nutty-tasting ancient grain that hails from Africa. This nutritional powerhouse is rich in amino acids, iron, calcium, and a type of fiber known as resistant starch (meaning it's a starch our body can't digest) that is believed to aid in weight management. I like to add ground teff to baked foods because the grain adds a great nutty flavor. The grain itself is a bit harder than wheat, so its flour adds a nice bite and toothsomeness.

I like the teff made by Bob's Red Mill.

CHIA EGG

Chia seeds and flax meal take on a sticky, gluey consistency when blended with a small amount of water. For that reason, these two ingredients can be used as egg replacements, and they help bind batter or dough. I've found chia binds a little bit more than flax, and so that's my go-to egg replacement, but I've given you a flax egg variation as well.

MAKES ENOUGH TO REPLACE 1 CHICKEN EGG

1 tablespoon chia seeds
3 tablespoons cold filtered water

Combine the chia seeds and water in a small bowl and stir. Let the mixture sit, stirring occasionally, until the chia absorbs all the water and forms a thick gel-like mass, about 20 minutes. Use immediately, adding to recipes as directed.

Variations

FLAX EGG: If you don't need as much binding in a recipe, but want a bit of moisture, try using a flax egg instead. Follow the procedure above, substituting flax meal for the chia.

EGGSTRA-STRENGTH CHIA OR FLAX EGG: If you're preparing a dish that needs more binding strength, try cutting back the water by half (that is, use 1 tablespoon chia seeds or flax meal to $4\frac{1}{2}$ teaspoons water).

Goji Berries

Goji berries are bittersweet-tasting, pill-size red berries commonly sold in dried form. They can be eaten cooked, raw, or dried, and today they are frequently added atop smoothie bowls and mixed into granola. Traditionally, goji berries were favored in Chinese medicine as a longevity aid. Goji berries contain antioxidants, vitamins, fiber, and minerals and are lauded for a wide array of nutritional benefits, including mood elevation and anti-inflammation. They're also believed to increase energy levels and defend against Alzheimer's, and their amino acids and antioxidants help combat free radicals and are a great skin food.

The first few times I tried goji berries I didn't really like the taste because of their tannic nature. But I changed my opinion after trying the kind packaged by Dragon Herbs (available at the company's online store and on Amazon.com), which are sweet and chewy and taste almost like candy, although they contain no added sugar.

Hemp Seeds

Hemp seeds, sometimes called *hemp hearts*, are actually tiny fruits with a grassy flavor and a hard outer shell similar to a sunflower seed. Hemp "seeds" come from the hemp plant, or *Cannabis sativa* L., but these seeds will not get you high! While hemp and marijuana plants are members of the same family, the two botanicals are quite different, mainly due to their level of THC, the psychoactive chemical that gets you stoned. (While the hemp plant contains very little THC—according to Colorado law, hemp must contain less than 0.3 percent—marijuana plants contain, on average, 5 to 30 percent THC.) Hemp seeds are high in amino acids and essential fatty acids, and they can be sprinkled on breakfast bowls, salads, or blended with water into alternative milks.

My preferred hemp brand is Navitas Organics, which is sold via their online store and also online at Amazon.com.

Hibiscus

Hibiscus, which goes by the name *jamaica* in Mexico (where it is quite popular in a tealike beverage), is a tropical flower that grows in a rainbow of colors, but it's the red-hued flowers that most commonly appear in foods and beverages. The dried flower is brewed into a deep pink tea that's high in antioxidants and tastes of red berries, with a sour, tannic finish. Hibiscus is celebrated for its nutritional benefits and is believed to combat high blood pressure and high cholesterol.

At home, I drop dried hibiscus flowers into a liter of cold filtered water and drink it throughout the day; for this book I've created a spiffed-up riff on cold brewed hibiscus tea that incorporates cinnamon and vanilla (see page 39).

I like to purchase organic dried hibiscus from Amazon.com.

Maca

Maca root, which grows in Peru, is considered an adaptogen, meaning it's an ingredient that helps the body cope with outside stress without compromising one's immune system. Maca, an off-white powder made from the ground, dried root of the maca plant, counts a long history in Andean culture, where it has been consumed for its ability to boost energy, balance hormones, and improve sexual function. In Peru, maca is also considered an aphrodisiac, and I've even seen the powder marketed there as a natural form of Viagra. Maca has a pleasant malty, earthy flavor that's great in drinks and added to baked goods. Sometimes I add a teaspoon of maca powder to my morning coffee as an energy booster.

My preferred maca brand is Navitas Organics.

Matcha

Matcha, which hails from Japan, is a finely milled, highly caffeinated powder made from green tea leaves. Traditionally, matcha powder is whisked with water to make a bright green tea–based drink with a grassy-sweet flavor. Matcha differs from regular green tea in that it's essentially a solution of tea leaves and water, meaning you're drinking the entire leaf and getting more of its nutrients than you do from regular green tea, which is the product of steeping the leaves in water. Thanks to its zippy green color, matcha is high in antioxidants, and, beyond its application as a tea, you'll find the powder incorporated into desserts and sometimes savory dishes, too. While I frequently drink matcha in place of coffee, for this book I've included a slew of sweet recipes that incorporate this neon green powder.

It's worthwhile to note that matcha powder comes in various grades (and as a result, at various price points). I've found that the pricier, higher-quality grades are sweeter, with more umami, while the lower-quality

grades often have a bitter flavor. While I always try to cook with and drink high-quality matcha powder, when baking, if you don't want to splurge on a can, it's alright to use a lower grade. But when drinking the tea straight, I'd suggest spending a bit more for a higher-quality powder.

I source matcha from the Brooklyn-based Japanese tea company Kettl, and from the Kyoto-based Ippodo, which sells via its own online store.

Medicinal Mushrooms

Medicinal mushrooms are having a moment—and I am not talking about the magical kind. While mushrooms have been consumed for their medicinal properties for centuries in various parts of the world, like China, it's only recently that Americans are catching on to these fungi's powerful health benefits. Considered adaptogens and anti-inflammatories (see opposite page), medicinal mushrooms help the body cope with external stressors without compromising the immune system. Experts say that consuming small doses of the mushrooms over the course of your life will improve your overall health (it takes about two months for the mushrooms' health benefits to kick in). Since medicinal mushrooms are sold in powder form, it's easy to add them to drinks or incorporate them into baked goods (on their own they have a sort of earthy, musty, woodsy flavor).

All of the mushrooms mentioned here—chaga, cordyceps, and reishi—are part of the "adaptogen" family, but each has its own host of more specific benefits. While these mushrooms can be pricey, you only take or use $\frac{1}{2}$ teaspoon to 1 teaspoon daily, so a small jar should last a decent amount of time. I like to add these mushrooms to my morning coffee, because the strong brew masks the mushrooms' earthy taste. You can also add them to a variety of dishes—but I'd caution you to add them to foods that already are rich in flavor, otherwise the mushrooms will take over.

I buy medicinal mushrooms from brands like Moon Juice and Sun Potion.

CHAGA: Considered the king of mushrooms, chaga is a healing mushroom that acts as an adaptogen, helping to keep the body's immune functions strong even during stressful situations. Chaga works to bring the body into balance. It's also high in antioxidants and B vitamins, and is a source of energy. Chaga has a woodsy flavor and is often sold as a powder, tea, or tincture.

CORDYCEPS: While reishi and chaga both grow on wood, cordyceps are a type of fungus that grows on the backs of caterpillars in high-altitude regions such as the Himalayas. In fact, cordyceps act as parasites, eventually consuming most of the host insect. Also an adaptogenic mushroom believed to increase longevity, cordyceps boost immunity, fight free radicals in the body, combat inflammation, and are tied to improved athletic endurance and heightened energy. Cordyceps have a woodsy flavor and are often sold as a powder or tincture.

REISHI: Reishi is believed to boost energy, lower blood pressure, fight inflammation, and strengthen the body against cancer and other diseases. Reishi has a woodsy flavor and is often sold as a powder, tea, or tincture.

Miso

Miso is a traditional Japanese paste made from soybeans that have been mixed with salt and koji (a type of mold also used to make sake). However, you can also find miso made from barley, rice, and other grains, sometimes with spice and citrus like yuzu added in. Miso comes in a variety of colors and flavors, with hues ranging from white and yellow to brown and red and flavors from sweet to meaty to spicy. In general, lighter color misos are milder in flavor, but all are rich in umami. Miso is most commonly found in the United States in soup form, but it's a wonderful multipurpose condiment that adds a savory flavor to sauces and dressings, and is also delicious as a dip for crudités. As a fermented food, miso is a great natural source of probiotics.

Nuts and Nut Milks

ALMONDS, ALMOND FLOUR, AND ALMOND MEAL: Of all the ingredients I use in this book, the organic almond is the one that comes into play most often. As a nut, almond imparts a distinctly clean, nutty, slightly roasted flavor that makes an excellent base for nut milks. As health food, organic raw almonds are loaded with healthy fats and contain protein and fiber, in addition to vitamin E, magnesium, and other essential minerals. Almonds enrich our hair and nails, regulate cholesterol, and reduce the risk of heart disease. Two of the most common ingredients in sweet and savory vegan cookery are almond flour and almond meal, both of which are high-protein, low-carb, and gluten-free. Though they are often used interchangeably, there is a difference between the two: Almond flour is made from finely ground blanched, skinned almonds; almond meal is made from finely ground raw almonds whose skins are left intact. Typically, almond flour is ground a bit finer than almond meal, and it has a slightly more unified texture since the nuts' skins have been removed. In terms of flavor, almond meal is a bit nuttier since the skins are incorporated.

I add almond meal to many of my recipes—I like its rougher texture and nuttiness. In baking, almond meal adds moisture and richness, though it can also make baked goods a bit dense. While almond meal and almond flour are quite easy to find at grocery stores, you can also make your own at home.

CASHEWS: Cashews are, surprisingly, not nuts but the seeds from the cashew fruit. Thanks to their subtle, sweet flavor and smooth, creamy texture, cashews are a staple in raw-vegan desserts. Blended cashews yield exceptionally smooth and rich milks, and when mixed with coconut oil produce a silky cream. Though lower in fiber than other nuts, cashews are also lower in fat, and much of the fat they do contain is monounsaturated—the type that doctors believe is good for your heart. Beyond containing less fat than almost all other nuts, cashews are rich in vitamin B_6 and the minerals potassium and magnesium.

HAZELNUTS: I absolutely adore the nutty flavor of hazelnuts. And when made into a milk (see page 33), hazelnut is the perfect flavor pairing with coffee. In terms of nutrition, these nuts (also sometimes called filberts) contain iron, fiber, potassium, magnesium, in addition to vitamins. In terms of healthy fat, hazelnuts contain more than almonds and pistachios, but less than walnuts and Brazil nuts. When

I shop for hazelnuts, I buy raw and organic whenever possible. I don't necessarily have a preferred brand, but I often buy bags of nuts from the fruit, grain, and seed bins at health food stores.

MACADAMIA NUTS: Despite the fact that they're high in both calories and fat, I love macadamia nuts' clean, buttery, sweet flavor. While macadamias contain more fat than any other common nut, the good news is that most of that fat is in the form of monounsaturated fatty acids—the kind of fat that helps reduce cholesterol and is beneficial for the heart. Macadamia nuts also contain iron, protein, and other vitamins and nutrients, and have been shown to aid in bone health, hormone regulation, and optimized brain function.

NUT MILKS: As their name suggests, nut milks are dairy alternative beverages made from a variety of nuts—they take on a creamy flavor akin to cow's milk. Generally, to make a nut milk, you soak nuts overnight, then blend them with water and other flavors like vanilla, and finally strain that mixture through a nut milk bag or cheesecloth.

You will find a range of nut milk recipes, and more detailed information on making them, on pages 27 to 37. When cooking, you can use homemade nut milks exactly as you would store-bought nut milks. Personally, I never buy commercial nut milks because they are filled with sugar, stabilizers, and other additives. But if you don't want to make your own nut milk at home, I'd advise seeking one out from a local farmers' market or searching for the most artisanal brand you can find. If you're allergic to nuts, you can always sub in other alt-milks like coconut milk, oat milk, or hemp milk.

Pearl Powder

Pearl powder is exactly what it sounds like—a fine powder made from pearls. Rich in amino acids and minerals such as magnesium, pearl powder has long been incorporated into Chinese medicine where it's consumed as a beauty tonic and believed to reverse the signs of aging, such as sun spots. I add pearl powder as a supplement to drinks.

Pink Himalayan Salt

While there's an endless variety of salts on the market in a rainbow of hues, at home I like to cook with mineral-rich pink Himalayan salt. Mined from the Punjab region of Pakistan, pink Himalayan salt—also known as pink salt—contains dozens of minerals, which are responsible for its rose-colored hue.

You can also sub in regular salt if you're not able to find pink Himalayan salt. However, it is now sold at Trader Joe's and even the commonly found spice brand McCormick sells its own.

Probiotics

Our gut is filled with "good" bacteria that help us absorb nutrients and combat infection, and new science is proving that these trillions of microorganisms can even have an impact on our mood. *Probiotics* is the marketing term for these wellness-promoting bacteria, which are found in products like yogurt and fermented foods. Probiotics are also sold as a loose powder, as pills, even in liquid form. Because probiotics are sensitive to heat, you'll want to store them in the fridge, and never add them to hot foods because the bacteria will die. I sometimes add a scoop of probiotic powder to cold smoothies, and I also add the powder to the breakfast custards starting on page 60.

Purple Yam

If there's one ingredient that's inspired me the most in cooking pretty plant-based foods, it's the bright purple yam, an ingredient I love for both its color and honey-sweet flavor. Rich in antioxidants thanks to its lavender hue, this root is incredibly versatile in cooking, and I use it to build everything from breakfast custard (see page 61) to a filling for tacos. Purple yams are sold fresh at natural foods markets like Whole Foods.

Sesame Seeds and Tahini

Especially popular in Mediterranean cuisine and Ayurvedic practices, these tiny seeds have a nutty, savory flavor. They're rich in oil and essential fatty acids, high in protein, and contain nutrients like magnesium. They've been linked to lowering blood pressure and cholesterol. Sesame seeds can be either black or white—the black version is simply unhulled white seeds. When sesame seeds—raw or roasted—are turned into a paste, they become tahini. I like to add tahini to baked goods for moisture and richness, and I also like to dip dried fruit into tahini as a snack, and spread it on rice cakes with a touch of raw honey.

My preferred tahini brand is Soom, which is sold at Whole Foods and online.

Sweeteners

Sugar is sugar is sugar. Meaning, regardless of the source—maple syrup, honey, processed cane sugar—the following sweeteners are still sweeteners and are thus not the best for you. If you're going to cook with a sweetener, firstly you should avoid anything that's not natural or contains ingredients you can't pronounce. Then, on the subject of wholesome sweeteners, why not take in some extra vitamins and minerals while you're at it? That's why, when it comes to sweeteners, I shy away from white table sugar, which contains zero nutritional benefits. Instead, I sub in coconut palm sugar, honey, maple syrup, and more. All of those ingredients are, yes, sweet, but they also all contain extra health-promoting nutrients. Like any sweetener, you should still consume them in moderation.

COCONUT NECTAR AND COCONUT PALM SUGAR: See page 9.

DATES: I use dates to sweeten most of my nut milks. And while different date species have slightly different flavor nuances, pretty much any type of date will do. I like dates because of their rich caramel flavor, and they also add a bit of body to nut milks. Since you're adding in the whole (pitted) dried fruit, you're getting fiber, in addition to a slew of vitamins and minerals such as copper and magnesium. I also like to incorporate dates into baked goods because they add extra moisture, and dates mixed with various grains make a great base for raw dessert bars. When possible, I buy dates grown without pesticides, in bulk.

My preferred date brand is Shields Date Farm in Palm Springs, California.

On Agave and Stevia

These "natural" sweeteners have become popular in recent years, but I stay away from them. Agave may be marketed as natural because it's plant-derived, but it's actually highly processed. With regard to stevia, unless you are using the plant's leaf, it's pretty adulterated, too—most liquid and powder stevia sweeteners are created through chemical processes and can include additives like erythritol, dextrose, and other artificial sweeteners. (And while we're at it, let's not overlook artificial sweeteners made from chemicals. These are flat-out bad, and you'll never find them in this book.)

LUCUMA: Lucuma is an orange-fleshed fruit indigenous to Peru that's dried, turned into a powder, and used as a low-glycemic sweetener. While you can use it in drinks, I've found that you need to add a lot of the powder to get perceptible sweetness, and because the beautiful exotic caramel flavor of dried lucuma is extremely delicate, it gets lost when mixed with strong flavors. For that reason, I like to mix lucuma into foods with lighter flavors such as vanilla chia pudding.

My preferred lucuma brand is Moon Juice.

MAPLE SYRUP: Maple syrup is the sweet liquid made from the cooked sap of the maple tree. Maple syrup is divided into categories based on its color: Grade A (further classified as Light Amber, Medium Amber, Dark Amber) or Grade B, the darkest of them all. In general, the darker the color, the stronger the maple flavor. I personally like dark maple syrups.

Maple syrup is unrefined, and therefore contains antioxidants and minerals, making it a more nutritious sweetener as compared with white sugar. It's also lower on the glycemic index.

MESQUITE: While mesquite may conjure images of grilled meat, which is often smoked over the tree's wood, this light brown powder, with a rich caramel flavor, is made from the pods of the tree. It is used as a low-glycemic sweetener in smoothies, other drinks, and desserts. Mesquite is also high in protein, and contains magnesium, potassium, iron, and zinc.

My preferred mesquite brand is Moon Juice.

MONK FRUIT: Monk fruit—which is indigenous to Southeast Asia and also goes by the name *luo han guo*—has been getting quite a bit of attention recently for its use as a sweetener. Sold most commonly in powdered form, monk fruit is about 200 times sweeter than white cane sugar and contains zero calories. It's also believed to contain high levels of antioxidants. On its own, pure monk fruit powder is a great way to sweeten both foods and drinks, but be sure to read the label—many companies sell monk fruit powder with other additives, including a processed sugar substitute called erythritol. While some people claim that erythritol is totally safe to consume, I prefer to avoid unnatural, processed additives.

Monk fruit powder is often available at health food stores; when shopping for it, just make sure to look out for the pure stuff.

RAW HONEY: One of my favorite sweeteners, for pretty much anything from a smoothie to baked goods, is raw honey. Raw honey is honey that has not been pasteurized,

processed, or heated, so it retains its natural enzymes, vitamins, and nutrients. It is used for its many medicinal benefits: It has been shown to help balance hormones, improve immunity, boost libido, and fight allergies.

YACON SYRUP: This is a sweet, lightly caramel flavored, dark brown syrup that's made from the root of the yacon plant, which is indigenous to South America. I am a huge fan of yacon syrup because not only does it have a low glycemic index score, it has far fewer calories than other sweeteners like honey and maple syrup. This is because it contains something called indigestible inulin, which is a probiotic fiber that our bodies can't break down, so it passes right through the body. I love to use yacon syrup in everything from smoothies and coffee to baked goods.

You can buy yacon syrup at health food stores and natural foods supermarkets like Whole Foods (I like to source mine from Amazon.com because there it costs about half the price).

Tocos

Tocos, which stands for "tocotrienols," is a shimmery off-white dust that's derived from the nutrient-rich bran of brown rice. Thanks to its fat-soluble high vitamin E content, tocos is especially good for the skin and connective tissues, and is thus lauded as a beauty food. In terms of flavor, tocos tastes like a malted vanilla milkshake. It can be eaten in its raw state, mixed into drinks, or sprinkled onto oatmeal or chia pudding (see page 56). I add tocos to various drink recipes as a supplement (see page 35).

My preferred tocos brand is Sur Potion.

Turmeric

A vital ingredient in many Indian curries, turmeric—a plant that's part of the ginger family—boasts a beautiful neon yellow-orange hue and is consumed both fresh and in dried form. Most commonly, the earthy, peppery-flavored root is dried and ground into a powder, and that's the form I cook with in this book. Turmeric is believed to be one of the world's most powerful herbs thanks to its active compound curcumin (also present in cinnamon), with an ongoing list of health benefits that doctors continue to study. Turmeric is celebrated for its anti-inflammatory properties, and is believed to combat depression, help with cholesterol, and more. Turmeric is also high in manganese and iron. And thanks to its beautiful earthy yellow hue, it makes an awesome natural food dye (see page 23). Turmeric also works beautifully paired with sweet fruit flavors—I love to add it to beverages along with complementary tropical ingredients like coconut and mango (see page 44).

Vanilla

Cooking with fresh vanilla beans makes a huge difference in recipes as the bean's strong, pure flavor shines. (Bonus: Vanilla beans are rich in magnesium and potassium, too.) Since vanilla beans can be hugely expensive, I buy mine in bulk online from Heilala Vanilla, which sources from Tonga. After you've purchased fresh beans, make sure to store them in an airtight container to preserve their moisture; beans left open to the air will dry out. Also, if you scrape out seeds from a pod, you can reserve the pod for another use. For example, sometimes I store pods in a container of coconut palm sugar to imbue it with a subtle fragrance. Or you can also add a few pods to about 6 ounces of vodka to make your own homemade vanilla extract. Let that potion rest for a few months and voilà!

I also sometimes cook with vanilla powder and pure vanilla extract. Though the term "vanilla powder" can reference different vanilla products, the type I use is made from dried, ground vanilla beans. Regarding vanilla extract, I advise you to spend a bit more on a premium brand (make sure to read the label as some include sugar), especially when using it to make almond milk.

I like Heilala and Nielsen-Massey for both powder and extract.

How to UNICORN Your Food
#eatcolor

I always try to cook with the most naturally colorful foods because they are higher in antioxidants than those that are pale. Plus, colored foods look prettier on a plate! I've put together a list of the rainbow of ingredients that I incorporate into my cooking most often—foods that add both nutrition and color to an endless slew of dishes.

Pink and Red

Beets: Beets come in many different colors, but I usually cook with the common red-pink variety. In cases where you want to impart a beet's pink color but not its earthy flavor, you have a few options. You can make a dye from the vegetable (see page 23) and experiment with dip-dyeing or painting it onto ingredients like spring roll wrappers (see page 98) or vegetable slices (see page 135) for an ombre effect. Or try dropping various light-colored ingredients into the dye such as sliced onions, apples, and jicama. If you're looking to add a pink color to, say, almond milk (see page 28), your best bet is to drop a scrubbed raw beet into some hot water and allow the vegetable to stain the water magenta, then use that water, once cooled, as the liquid for blending the nuts. Since beets are extremely rich in color, size doesn't matter so much; even a small red beet can stain a few cups of water.

To color a larger amount of water—for example if you're cooking noodles or rice—place the desired amount of water in a pot, add one whole medium-size scrubbed, unpeeled, raw beet, and bring the water to boil. Once the water reaches a boil, remove the beet with a slotted spoon, and cook your noodles or rice in the tinted water as directed.

I also sometimes use beet powder, made from dehydrated, ground beets, to add color to a dish. I like to stir it into puddings, blend it into nut milks, and even use it to stain fennel slices pink (see page 135). I buy the powder at Kalustyan's, an Indian and Middle Eastern specialty food market in New York (kalustyans.com).

Finally, if you're looking to add both color *and* flavor to a dish, such as waffles (see page 67), soups, hummus (see page 118) or other bean dips, then I'd suggest making a beet puree (see the technique on page 68) and adding it incrementally until your desired effects are achieved.

Dried goji berries: These little bittersweet berries are an earthy red; I use them as a garnish.

Hibiscus flowers: Soak a handful of hibiscus flowers in a cup of warm or room temperature water and you'll be left with a dark pink liquid that you can use in beverages or in a similar fashion to the beet dye (see above).

Pitaya powder: This is made from freeze-dried pitaya fruit (aka dragon fruit) and imparts a vibrant pink color when stirred into beverages, puddings, ice creams, and more. You can also sprinkle it on dishes as a garnish for just a pop of pink.

Raspberries: While I incorporate fresh raspberries into my cooking for flavor and as a garnish, I am especially keen on freeze-dried raspberries for their magenta color. I like to crumble the berries into a coarse powder with my fingers and use it as a garnish.

Rose petals: You can use fresh and/or dried rose petals as a garnish on various dishes.

Purple

Purple cabbage: As with beets, when you boil this cabbage in water, the vegetable's pigment leaches into the water, staining it dark purple. While you can certainly put the cooked cabbage in a blender or food processor and turn it into a colored puree, if you're looking to add color rather than flavor, use the stained water instead. The purple water can be added to savory dishes like soups and dips.

Yellow

Bee pollen: Sprinkle these crunchy, mildly sweet granules on a variety of dishes (or use them as a coating) for a hit of bright yellow.

Turmeric: Dried ground turmeric boasts a beautiful mustard-yellow hue. Simply mix a small amount of the powder into white foods such as cooked rice, cauliflower rice, and nut milks to stain them yellow. But note that turmeric channels a strong earthy, spicy flavor—use a light touch.

Green

Matcha powder: As I mentioned on page 14, not all matcha is created equal. The color of the green tea is directly related to quality and price. A cheap matcha will look brown-green, while a pricier one will take on more of a neon green. Of course, matcha stains beverages a grassy color, but if you mix the powder into foods (like Matcha Cookies with Cardamom, Orange, and Toasted Pistachios, page 130), the food will become green, too. I also coat seeds and nuts in matcha powder to create unique garnishes with a pop of color and crunch. To make matcha-dusted seeds or nuts, simply toss 2 tablespoons seeds or toasted chopped nuts with ¼ to ½ teaspoon of matcha powder to coat.

Pistachios: Use chopped or whole toasted pistachios as a bright green garnish on an array of different dishes.

Spirulina: Mix ¼ teaspoon of this deep green algae powder into a half cup of chia pudding, and you'll quickly have a colorful snack. You can also add spirulina powder to a drink for color, and sprinkle it atop salads and veggies for a green twist.

I also love spirulina crunchies—which are little Grape-Nutlike algae clusters—sprinkled atop salads, soups, and roasted veggies for a health boost, toothsome crunch, and colorful garnish.

Blue

Blue Majik: This algae powder gives foods a cool turquoise color without affecting their flavor. Mix ½ teaspoon or more into drinks and foods until the desired blue is reached.

Blueberries: My Lisa Frank Mountain Cake (page 141) serves as a great example of the purple-blue color blueberries impart to a dish. To get that added color, you simply need to puree blueberries with other ingredients. Of course, blueberries also make a great garnish on their own, frozen, fresh, or freeze-dried.

Additional Unicorn Garnishes

Cacao nibs, chia seeds, coconut flakes, edible flowers, hemp seeds, flaxseeds, pepitas, chopped nuts, white and black sesame seeds

NATURAL RAINBOW SPRINKLES

MAKES 3 CUPS

Ever since I was a kid I've loved rainbow sprinkles. I haven't found a (truly) natural brand on the market that I like, so I usually just make my own at home. And it's so easy to do! All you need is 3 cups of shredded, unsweetened coconut and a few colorful ingredients. The basic idea is to make a dye from a colorful ingredient by mixing it with boiling or room-temperature water, depending on the ingredient. Once you have that dye, you can mix a few drops with a bit of shredded coconut and pop the coconut in the oven (or a dehydrator) to dry it out. I don't have a dehydrator, so I just make my sprinkles in the oven and toast them at a low temperature for about an hour or until they feel dry.

To make the dyes

<u>Bright blue-green</u>: Stir 1 teaspoon Blue Majik into ¼ cup lukewarm water.

<u>Bright pink</u>: Stir ¼ cup dried hibiscus flowers into ¼ cup lukewarm water.

<u>Green</u>: Stir ¾ teaspoon spirulina powder into ¼ cup lukewarm water.

<u>Magenta</u>: Add 1 whole, scrubbed (unpeeled) beet to 1 cup boiling water and let steep.

<u>Purple-Blue</u>: Boil 1 cup water with 1 cup chopped purple cabbage.

<u>Yellow-gold</u>: Stir 1 teaspoon ground turmeric into ¼ cup lukewarm water.

To make the sprinkles

1. Preheat the oven to the lowest temperature.
2. Divide 3 cups shredded, unsweetened coconut among six small bowls (or fewer if you plan to use fewer colors). Working one bowl at a time, drop a small amount of the first dye onto the coconut and stir; add a bit more dye if needed to reach the desired color (you don't want the coconut to be very wet; use just enough dye to tint it). Repeat with the remaining bowls of coconut and the remaining dyes until each bowl of coconut is tinted a different color.
3. Spread out the tinted coconut in a single layer on a rimmed baking sheet (or two), being sure to keep the different colors separate. Bake until the coconut is completely dry to the touch, about 1 hour.
4. Let cool completely, then transfer the coconut sprinkles to an airtight container to combine.

Natural Rainbow Sprinkles will keep, in an airtight container at room temperature, for up to 1 month.

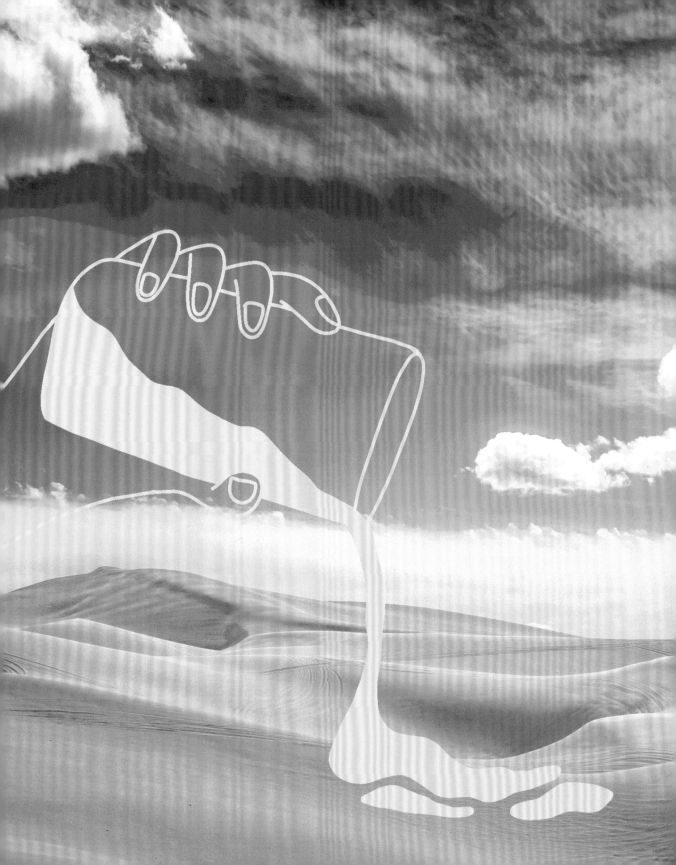

Two

UNICORN MILKS + OTHER DRINKS

Vanilla Bean–Almond Milk

Black Sesame Horchata

Cardamom-Rose Milk

Hazelnut Milk

Goji Coconut Cashew Milk

Malted Majik Milk

Pineapple, Ginger, and Basil Matcha Juice

Cold Brewed Hibiscus-Cinnamon Iced Tea

This Is *Not* Blue Gatorade

Frozen Turmeric Lassi

The Hot Green Smoothie

Babi's Cold Kicker

Toasted Coconut Cold Brew

Begin every morning with a drink.

Sometimes that morning pick-me-up involves coffee, other times matcha. But regardless of the flavor of my caffeine delivery, it always includes a splash of whatever nut milk I have in my fridge.

The kernel of inspiration behind this book in its entirety stems from my love for the flavor of vanilla bean. The very first nut milk I ever made—years ago in my Santa Monica, California, kitchen—was flavored vanilla bean–almond, and from there, after throwing in dates and a pinch of salt, I was quickly hooked on the drink's milkshake-esque flavor. Fast-forward a year and I found myself in my Manhattan kitchen whipping up almond milk—since I could find zero natural options at local markets—adding a pinch of spirulina and spice to give the milk a lightly exotic kick and unexpected green hue. I played around with passion fruit, turmeric, goji . . . cashews, pumpkin seeds . . . and one day, I looked down at four milks I had created in a pastel rainbow of white, pink, yellow, and green. They reminded me of a unicorn's mane . . . and the name *Unicorn Milk* was born.

This chapter includes my original Unicorn Milk recipe (page 28), plus other colorful (and healthful!) alt-milks. You can make these recipes to be consumed as is, or you can build them into dishes that come later in this book. There are also refreshing beverages like a play on a mango lassi (page 44), a deep purple elixir that will help kick a hangover (page 42), and a spiffed-up take on a classic Mexican tea (page 39).

A Note on Almond Milks

It is worth every amount of the minimal effort needed to make your own almond milks—they are beyond delicious and light-years better than the supermarket stuff, which is heaped with sugar and artificial ingredients. But before you jump in, please heed this advice:

• My base almond milk recipe (see page 28), which is the foundation of numerous other Unicorn Milks in this book, incorporates vanilla bean. The quality of your vanilla bean (or vanilla extract) needs to be high. If you use a poor-quality vanilla, the milk just won't taste as good. My personal favorite is Heilala vanilla beans from Tonga (which you can buy online), but if you don't want to take that step, Nielsen-Massey is a quality brand available at many supermarkets.

• The reason so many "house-made" almond milks at cafés taste like water is because the water-to-nut ratio is off. I like a richer, whole milk–style almond milk, so I use a ratio of about 5:2 water to nuts. You can play around with this ratio depending on how rich you want your milk to be.

• Almond milk should be made with raw almonds—to whatever extent possible, make sure you're buying raw and not pasteurized (see The Raw Truth about Raw Almonds), and always buy organic.

• The reason you soak almonds is both to soften them for blending, and because soaking the nuts "sprouts" them. Almonds contain natural enzymes that are dormant while the almond is in its dry state. Soaking the nuts activates their enzymes and increases their vitamin content, making the nuts—and the resulting milk—more healthful.

• Invest in a nut milk bag! While you can use cheesecloth to strain your milks, bags work better because they hold in all of the milk and nut particles without the worry of the milk spilling out. Nut milk bags are supercheap, about $6, and can be bought online and at some grocery stores.

• And finally, blending your milk will require a relatively high-powered blender. In my experience, the motors in inexpensive blenders aren't strong enough to break down the almonds, and therefore the milk never gets creamy. You don't necessarily need a VitaMix, which is what I use and recommend, but if you make almond milk and notice that your almonds remain in pieces that look like grains of sand, then that's a sign you need a stronger blender.

The Raw Truth about Raw Almonds

Contrary to what you might think, raw almonds are often not raw at all. In 2007, the USDA banned the sale of *truly* raw almonds, meaning that almonds sold in this country must be heat-pasteurized or fumigated with propylene oxide gas (PPO), a known carcinogen. Many believe this pasteurization process negatively affects an almond's flavor. The silver lining is that there's a loophole. A farmer in the United States can sell direct to consumers, in small amounts, almonds that have not been pasteurized or fumigated. You can search via the internet for almond farms in California, and farms that don't treat their nuts in any way will usually say so on their website.

On another note, almonds imported from countries like Italy and Spain *can* actually be raw. Just look for the almonds' country of origin on the package—if they are described as raw nuts from Italy or Spain, it's likely that they are, in fact, untreated. I've also noticed that some brands will add the words "truly raw" as opposed to just "raw," and those almonds tend not to be treated.

VANILLA BEAN–ALMOND MILK

It all started with this simple drink—the first Unicorn Milk. It's extra rich in deep vanilla flavor, with a hint of caramel from the dates. I've made this milkshake-flavored recipe now hundreds of times—it is a staple in my fridge. If you are intimidated by the notion of making your own almond milk, don't be. It really couldn't be easier. Just be sure to read A Note on Almond Milks (page 27) before you dive in.

MAKES ABOUT 2½ CUPS

1 cup organic, raw almonds

2½ cups filtered water

1 vanilla bean (see Note), plus extra as needed

1 large pitted date, plus extra as needed

Pinch of salt (I like pink Himalayan salt), plus extra as needed

1. Place the almonds in a medium bowl and cover with tap water to a depth of about 1 inch. Let soak overnight or for up to 2 days; the almonds will puff up as they absorb water.

2. Drain and rinse the almonds and transfer them to a high-powered blender, along with the filtered water, vanilla bean, date, and salt. Blend on high speed until the almonds are completely broken down, about 30 seconds.

3. Position a medium bowl under a nut milk bag and pour the almond milk mixture into the bag. Holding the top of the bag shut with hand, use the other to squeeze the almond milk from the pulp until it's dry (reserve the pulp for another use—see pages 110 to 112; it will keep, in an airtight container in the refrigerator, for up to 4 days). Taste the milk. If it is not sweet enough (I like it just barely sweet), or if the flavor needs to be adjusted, pour the milk back into the blender and add more date, salt, or vanilla to taste.

Vanilla Bean–Almond Milk will keep, covered and refrigerated, for about 5 days.

Note: If you can't find fresh vanilla beans, sub in 2 teaspoons pure vanilla extract.

A study in black and white:
Black Sesame Horchata
(page 30) and Vanilla
Bean–Almond Milk

BLACK SESAME HORCHATA

After researching variations of horchata—a creamy, sweet rice- and almond-based drink—I learned that in some parts of the world, like Puerto Rico, it is made with sesame seeds in place of rice. I've always loved the savory flavor of black sesame, especially in ice cream, so I immediately started thinking that black sesame might make for an interesting nut milk flavor. This black sesame horchata is as good as I hoped it would be.

Since black sesame carries a strong savory flavor, you need to up the sweetness for balance. When making this recipe, you'll have a bit of extra sesame milk left over. I like to take that milk and add chia seeds, oats, unsweetened shredded coconut, and flax meal, mix it up, and leave it in the fridge to make overnight oats.

MAKES ABOUT 1¾ CUPS

½ cup black sesame seeds

1¼ cups filtered water

1 tablespoon raw honey, plus extra as needed

1 cup Vanilla Bean–Almond Milk (page 28)

¾ teaspoon ground cinnamon

1. Place the sesame seeds in a small bowl and add tap water to cover to a depth of about 1 inch. Let soak overnight.

2. Drain and rinse the sesame seeds. Transfer them to a high-powered blender and add the filtered water and honey. Blend on high speed until the sesame seeds are completely broken down, about 2 minutes.

3. Position a medium bowl under a nut milk bag and pour the sesame seed milk mixture into the bag. Holding the top of the bag with one hand, use the other hand to squeeze the sesame seed milk from the pulp (reserve the pulp for another use—see pages 110 to 112; it will keep, in an airtight container in the refrigerator, for up to 4 days).

4. Rinse out the blender and pour ¾ cup of the sesame seed milk back in, setting aside the remaining milk for another use (you will have about 1 cup of milk left over; it will keep, in an airtight container in the refrigerator, for 4 days). Add the almond milk and cinnamon and blend to combine, 15 seconds. Taste the horchata. If it is not sweet enough (I like it just barely sweet), add more honey as needed.

Black Sesame Horchata will keep, covered and refrigerated, for up to 5 days.

CARDAMOM-ROSE MILK

I am hugely inspired by the 5,000-year-old Indian tradition of natural healing known as Ayurveda, a belief system that considers food to be medicine. I am likewise hugely inspired by Indian cuisine, and its beautiful array of bold flavors and colors. Two of my favorite Indian dessert ingredients are rose and cardamom, so I decided to combine them into a milk. I love this pale pink milk for its delicate, elegant flavor. You can drink it as is, or mix it with oats for a warming morning meal. Or, drop in a spoonful of chia seeds to turn it into a killer chia pudding, then top it with chopped pistachios for extra color and crunch.

This milk tastes softly of rose, but if you find that the flavor isn't coming through to your liking, you can blend more rose petals into the mix, or add a couple drops of food-grade rose extract (just use a light hand—you want to boost the flavor without it tasting like you're drinking a bottle of perfume).

MAKES ABOUT 2½ CUPS

1 recipe Vanilla Bean–Almond Milk (page 28)

3 tablespoons dried rose petals (see Note)

1 teaspoon ground cardamom

Combine the milk, rose petals, and cardamom in a high-powered blender. Blend on high speed until the rose petals are completely broken down and the milk is pale pink, about 30 seconds. Transfer the milk to a glass jar with a lid, and keep it sealed in the fridge.

Cardamom-Rose Milk will keep, covered and refrigerated, for up to 5 days.

Note: Dried rose petals come in varying degrees of flavor, and there's no surefire way to know how strong the petals will taste until you try them. Your best bet is to buy from a reputable spice market, which is what I do. I source my rose petals from SOS Chefs in New York City, and the jars I buy there are super fragrant—probably more so than most brands. However, you can also find dried rose petals online at Amazon.com (just make sure they're food-grade and organic).

Make It Magical
Add 1 teaspoon pearl powder with the other ingredients.

HAZELNUT MILK

'll admit it. In college, I drank flavored coffee. One of my best friends, Rebecca, got me hooked on hazelnut coffee, and I drank it with abandon for four years of my life. Upon graduating, though, without the need for weekly Dunkin' Donuts visits (LA and NYC offer far more quality-minded coffee operations), I switched over to a purer brew. But ultimately, the flavors of coffee and hazelnuts pair beautifully, and this here hazelnut milk is one of my favorite ways to add a bit of nuance to a cup of coffee—naturally, of course.

1. Place the hazelnuts in a medium bowl and add tap water to cover to a depth of about 1 inch. Let soak overnight.

2. Drain and rinse the hazelnuts. Transfer them to a high-powered blender. Add the filtered water, date, vanilla bean, and salt. Blend on high speed until the hazelnuts are completely broken down, about 1 minute.

3. Position a medium bowl under a nut milk bag and pour the hazelnut milk mixture into the bag.

Holding the top of the bag with one hand, use the other hand to squeeze the hazelnut milk from the pulp (reserve the pulp for another use—see pages 110 to 112; it will keep, in an airtight container in the refrigerator, for up to 4 days). Taste the milk. If it is not sweet enough (I like it just barely sweet), or the flavor needs to be adjusted, blend in more date, salt, or vanilla to taste.

Hazelnut Milk will keep, covered and refrigerated, for up to 5 days.

MAKES ABOUT 2 CUPS

1 cup raw hazelnuts, preferably organic

2½ cups filtered water

1 medium pitted date, plus extra as needed

½ vanilla bean (see Note, page 34), plus extra as needed

Pinch of salt (I like pink Himalayan salt), plus extra as needed

Note: If you can't find fresh vanilla beans, sub in 1 teaspoon pure vanilla extract.

Variation
Hazelnut-Cacao Milk: If you're a fan of cacao, you can add 5 teaspoons of cacao powder to the strained milk and reblend it to flip this into a hazelnut-cacao milk.

GOJI COCONUT CASHEW MILK

The best almond milk I've ever come across is in Venice, California. Jeff Leaf is the dude behind Mylkman, a local almond milk delivery company, and Jeff makes his almond milk using nuts blended with fresh coconut water. It's incredible. When I lived in LA, I used to buy jars of it, and I could barely get through a day without finishing it. The coconut water adds a soft sweetness to the milk, which beautifully complements the almond flavor. And that jar of deliciousness inspired me to consider making other milks with coconut water as a base.

Here, I'd suggest using fresh coconut water, but if you can't find it, your next best bet would be to use Harmless Harvest coconut water—it's a personal favorite.

MAKES ABOUT 1½ CUPS

½ cup raw cashews, preferably organic
1½ cups coconut water, preferably fresh
1 tablespoon goji berries
½ vanilla bean
Pinch of salt (I like pink Himalayan salt)

CASHEW!
BLESS YOU!

1. Put the cashews in a medium bowl and add tap water to cover to a depth of about 1 inch. Let soak overnight.

2. Drain and rinse the cashews. Transfer them to a high-powered blender, along with the coconut water, goji berries, vanilla bean, and salt. Blend on high speed until all the ingredients are completely broken down, about 30 seconds.

3. Position a medium bowl under a nut milk bag and pour the cashew milk mixture into the bag. Holding the top of the bag with one hand, use the other hand to squeeze the cashew milk from the pulp. (Since cashew nuts are rather soft, you'll have very little pulp left over in the nut milk bag.) Transfer the cashew milk to a glass jar with a lid, and keep it sealed in the fridge.

Goji Coconut Cashew Milk will keep, covered and refrigerated, for up to 5 days.

Pudding It! This milk makes an awesome chia pudding. Mix ½ cup Goji Coconut Cashew Milk with 2 tablespoons chia seeds in a small bowl and transfer it to the fridge to set for 30 minutes, stirring it every 10 minutes so the chia seeds don't stick together.

A Note on Water-to-Nut Ratios

You'll notice that my nut milk recipes (pages 28, 30, and 33) call for about 1 cup of nuts to 2½ cups of water (a ratio of 2:5), while this cashew milk recipe calls for only ½ cup of nuts to 1½ cups of water (a ratio of 1:3). That's because cashews are creamier than almonds, and therefore you can blend them with more water and still get a super-rich milk.

MALTED MAJIK MILK

The first blue-green milk I ever made was colored with spirulina, a protein- and nutrient-rich green algae, then spiced with cardamom and cinnamon. For this recipe I added a bit of adaptogenic maca root (see page 13) and vitamin-rich tocos (see page 19), both of which impart a sweet, malted flavor. The "Majik" in the name comes from a blue-pigmented extract of spirulina algae that's marketed as Blue Majik; it gives the milk a baby blue hue.

For a spicier version, add a pinch each of ground cardamom and cinnamon. You'll find that this milk tastes like a malted vanilla smoothie, so I like to drink it as is. And because it has energy-boosting maca, it's great in the morning or before a workout.

MAKES ABOUT 2½ CUPS
1 recipe Vanilla Bean–Almond Milk (page 28)
2 teaspoons maca powder
2 teaspoons tocos
¾ teaspoon Blue Majik (see Note)

Combine the milk, maca powder, tocos, and Blue Majik in a high-powered or standard blender. Blend on high speed until the powders are fully incorporated and the milk is pale blue, about 30 seconds. Transfer the milk to a glass jar with a lid, and keep sealed in the fridge.

Malted Majik Milk will keep, covered and refrigerated, for up to 5 days.

Note: If you can't find Blue Majik, sub in spirulina powder (just be aware that the color will be light green instead of blue).

Nut milks in the colors of a unicorn's mane
(from left to right): Cardamom-Rose
Milk (page 32), Goji Coconut Cashew
Milk (page 34), and Malted Majik Milk

PINEAPPLE, GINGER, AND BASIL MATCHA JUICE

Judging from the number of recipes in this book that incorporate matcha, you can probably tell that I'm somewhat taken with the bright green powder. It's true. I do love matcha. And in this refreshing drink, which you could easily freeze into an ice pop (see Pop It! below), matcha adds a savory, umami note to contrast the brightness of the pineapple and the freshness of the ginger. The basil leaves add a subtle spicy note for an overall tropical-tasting green juice. Heads up—this is the only drink for which you'll need a juicer!

MAKES ABOUT 1⅓ CUPS

4 cubes (about 1½ inches each) fresh pineapple
2 large pieces (about 8 ounces total) fresh, organic ginger
30 large fresh basil leaves
½ teaspoon matcha powder
Ice cubes, for serving

1. Pass the pineapple and ginger through a juicer.

2. Transfer the juice to a blender and add the basil leaves and matcha powder. Blend on high speed until the basil leaves are completely broken down and the juice is soft green, about 30 seconds.

3. Pour into a glass with ice and serve.

Pineapple, Ginger, and Basil Matcha Juice will keep, covered and refrigerated, for about 2 days.

Pop It! To turn this juice into ice pops, simply distribute the juice among your desired ice pop molds and freeze.

Make It Magical
Add 1 teaspoon chlorophyll to the blender in Step 2.

COLD BREWED HIBISCUS-CINNAMON ICED TEA

The first time I had iced jamaica tea was in Mexico. *Agua de jamaica*, which translates from Spanish to "hibiscus water," is a common beverage made from water, dried hibiscus flowers (see page 13), and sugar. With a tart flavor reminiscent of cranberries and a pretty purple-pink hue that indicates a high level of antioxidants, hibiscus water has since become a regular drink for me. At home I often just drop a handful of dried hibiscus flowers into a water bottle, shake it up, and drink the increasingly pink water throughout the day—something you should try, too. But here I've jazzed up the recipe a bit, adding a hit of cinnamon, some vanilla, a squeeze of lime, and a sprinkling of lime zest to brighten the drink.

MAKES ABOUT 4 CUPS

4 cups filtered water
½ cup (7.5 ounces) dried hibiscus flowers
5 teaspoons fresh lime juice
4 teaspoons pure maple syrup
1 teaspoon freshly grated lime zest
½ teaspoon ground cinnamon
⅛ teaspoon vanilla bean powder or ¼ teaspoon pure vanilla extract
Ice cubes, for serving

1. Pour the filtered water into a glass or plastic pitcher and add the hibiscus flowers. Transfer to the fridge and let infuse overnight.

2. Position a fine-mesh strainer over a blender and pour the hibiscus water through it; discard the flowers. Add the lime juice, maple syrup, lime zest, cinnamon, and vanilla and blend until combined, about 10 seconds. Pour into glasses with ice and serve.

Cold Brewed Hibiscus-Cinnamon Iced Tea will keep, in an airtight container in the refrigerator, for about 5 days.

Cool and quenching: This Is *Not* Blue Gatorade (page 42), Cold Brewed Hibiscus-Cinnamon Iced Tea (page 39), and Pineapple, Ginger, and Basil Matcha Juice (page 38)

THIS IS NOT BLUE GATORADE

In my regular day-to-day life, I don't drink soda or consume anything artificially colored or flavored. But when I'm hungover, there's only one cure: blue Gatorade. I cave in the hopes of feeling better—not only does Gatorade rehydrate the body, but it also contains important electrolytes that alcohol depletes. The thing is: It also contains a lot of less desirable stuff (like dyes and loads of sugar), so I've long wanted to create a natural hangover helper to consume in its place. (Note that I am not using the word *cure* or *remedy* here: There's no miracle fix for a hangover other than time, and what you're really looking for is to lessen whatever symptoms you're feeling.)

During a recent trip to Peru, I reacquainted myself with *chicha morada*, the ubiquitous, nutrient-rich drink made from purple Peruvian corn boiled with spices. It occurred to me, with regard to both flavor and color, that I could use chicha morada as the base for my hangover elixir. It turns out that purple corn is an excellent source of potassium and magnesium, in addition to a slew of other vitamins and minerals—exactly what your body needs after a night out. Furthermore, purple corn is high in anthocyanins, pigments that act like antioxidants and combat inflammation— another side effect of overindulging. So I combined the base flavors of chicha morada (purple corn, cinnamon, clove, pineapple, apple) with coconut water—a great source of potassium, magnesium, and electrolytes in its own right— and this delicious not-Gatorade was born.

I don't use sugar in this recipe because I think the pineapple and apple impart enough sweetness, but feel free to add coconut palm sugar or honey to taste.

1. Combine the filtered water, corn, cinnamon, cloves, pineapple, and apples in a large pot and cook on high heat until beginning to boil, about 7 minutes. Reduce the heat to medium and simmer, uncovered, until the liquid has reduced to about 3 cups, about 1 hour.

2. Position a strainer over a large, heat-resistant bowl and pour the purple corn mixture through it, separating the liquid from the solids; discard the solids. Pour the corn "juice" into a large glass bottle with a lid and add the coconut water and lime juice. Shake to combine the ingredients and season to taste with more lime juice and coconut palm sugar if you'd like.

3. Chill in the fridge or serve over ice.

This Is Not Blue Gatorade will keep, covered in the refrigerator, for up to 3 days.

Note: Purple corn kernels can be purchased online at Nuts .com.

MAKES ABOUT 3⅔ CUPS

1 gallon filtered water

3 cups purple corn kernels (about 15 ounces; see Note)

2 cinnamon sticks

1 teaspoon whole cloves

6 cups fresh pineapple chunks (about 1½ pounds or 1 whole pineapple)

2 medium apples, peeled, cored, and cut into ½-inch cubes

⅔ cup coconut water, preferably fresh

¼ cup fresh lime juice, plus extra as needed

Coconut palm sugar or raw honey (optional)

FROZEN TURMERIC LASSI

Milky golden drinks spiked with turmeric are everywhere these days, beloved for their exotic flavor and sunset-colored hue. Turmeric, a rhizome popular in Indian cuisine and traditional medicine, has recently become a darling of the American wellness world, lauded for its anti-inflammatory properties, among other benefits. Here, I spliced together a turmeric latte and a mango lassi—a common Indian refreshment made from mango, milk, and yogurt—to create one summer-friendly drink. Since mango lassis naturally contain probiotics from the yogurt, I added in a bit of probiotic powder (see page 17), plus coconut milk and avocado for richness.

SERVES 1

½ cup coconut milk

½ cup ice cubes, plus extra for serving

¼ ripe avocado, pitted and peeled

3 ounces frozen mango chunks

2 ounces frozen pineapple chunks

2 teaspoons raw honey

1 teaspoon freshly grated peeled ginger (from about 1-inch piece)

1 teaspoon ground turmeric

1 teaspoon probiotic powder

¾ teaspoon ground cardamom

¾ teaspoon ground cinnamon

⅛ teaspoon freshly ground black pepper

Pinch of ground cloves

Combine the coconut milk, ice cubes, avocado, mango, pineapple, honey, ginger, turmeric, probiotic powder, cardamom, cinnamon, pepper, and cloves in a blender and puree until smooth, about 30 seconds. Pour into a glass with ice and serve immediately.

THE HOT GREEN
SMOOTHIE

I lived in Santa Monica, California, for three years, and during that period a wellness café named Kye's opened. The first time I went in, I tried a green drink called Ayurvedic One-A-Day, and I was immediately hooked. I asked the owner, Jeanne Cheng, for the recipe and she happily shared it. This is my tweaked take on it (I removed a few ingredients for a simplified version)—a cross between a green smoothie and a bright and savory soup. I am somewhat addicted to this drink. It's a perfect, and delicious, way to stock up on green things.

1 tablespoon coconut oil

5 asparagus stalks, ends trimmed

1¼ cups filtered water

4 large kale leaves

2 Swiss chard leaves

½ cup packed fresh spinach leaves

½ cup packed fresh flat-leaf (Italian) parsley leaves

½ cup packed fresh cilantro leaves

¼ cup raw cashews, preferably organic

1 teaspoon fresh lemon juice

½ teaspoon coarse sea salt

1. Heat the coconut oil in a medium pot over medium heat. Add the asparagus and stir to coat in the oil, then add ½ cup of the filtered water. Cover and cook until the asparagus begins to brown, about 4 minutes. Stir in the kale, Swiss chard, and spinach, cover, and cook until the greens have wilted slightly and are bright green, about 5 minutes. Remove from the heat.

2. Stir in the parsley and cilantro, cover, and let rest, 2 minutes. Transfer the green mixture to a high-powered blender and add the cashews, lemon juice, salt, and remaining ¾ cup of filtered water. Blend until smooth, about 45 seconds.

3. Pour into mugs and drink immediately.

BABI'S COLD KICKER

When I was growing up, anytime I felt under the weather, my Czech grandmother *Babi* (that's Czech for "grandma") would make me a batch of honey-lemon-ginger tea. It was a simple recipe without any measurements. Because that's how grandmothers are, right? They make recipes by feel. Babi would add a bit of water to a pot, squeeze in the juice from a lemon and drop the fruit in whole, add a knob of fresh ginger, then honey to taste. She'd boil the whole thing for about 10 minutes then serve the scalding mixture to me in a mug—and it would inevitably burn the roof of my mouth, but always make me feel better.

Because Babi doesn't have a proper recipe for this drink, I've remade it myself, this time with measurements and all. The basic ratio here is 1 cup of water to 1 lemon to 1 tablespoon of honey plus a thumb-size knob of fresh ginger. Although my version doesn't call for adding the whole lemon out of fear there might be pesticides on the fruit's skin, if you're buying organic lemons from the farmers' market or, even better, plucking them off your own tree, I'd suggest going for it.

MAKES ABOUT 3½ CUPS

4 cups filtered water

Juice of 4 lemons

¼ cup raw honey, or to taste

1 piece (5 inches long by 1 inch thick) fresh ginger, peeled, roughly cut into ½-inch-thick pieces (about 1¼ ounces)

¼ or ½ ounce fresh ginger juice (optional, for an added kick)

1. Combine the filtered water, lemon juice, honey, and ginger in a medium pot over medium heat and simmer until you begin to smell the honey, about 10 minutes. Remove from the heat and let cool for 3 minutes.

2. Stir in the ginger juice, if using, then pour into mugs and serve immediately.

TOASTED COCONUT COLD BREW

I have this obsession with combining the flavors of coconut and coffee. Coffee made from coconut water, a shot of espresso poured into a fresh coconut, coffee mixed with coconut cream . . . I just love it. In my morning cup of coffee, when I don't have any fresh nut milk at home, I add a scoop of coconut oil—it serves to impart a creaminess to the brew without making it too heavy.

Since I was a kid, I've always loved coconut, especially toasted shredded coconut. So, I decided that someone needed to make a toasted coconut cold brew, and I decided that person should be me. I've tried making cold brew at home, adding a cup of unsweetened shredded coconut to the overnight steep—and that works, but the flavor is subtle. For a richer toasted coconut flavor, you can just go ahead and add a tablespoon of toasted shredded coconut to the coffee and then blend. My recipe, below.

SERVES 1

1 tablespoon unsweetened shredded coconut
½ cup cold-brew coffee (my favorite brands are Stumptown and Blue Bottle)
½ cup coconut or almond milk
2 teaspoons coconut nectar or coconut palm sugar
Ice cubes, for serving
Coconut Whip (page 169), for garnish (optional)

1. Preheat the oven to 350°F.

2. Spread the shredded coconut out on a rimmed baking sheet and toast it in the oven until golden brown, about 5 minutes. (Watch closely so the coconut doesn't burn.)

3. Combine the cold brew, coconut milk, toasted coconut, and coconut nectar in a blender and blend until combined, about 20 seconds. Pour the coconut cold brew into a tall glass with ice. Top with coconut whip, if desired, and serve.

Three

BRUNCH EVERY DAY

AM

Homemade Cinnamon Toast Crunch

Avo-Chia Brekkie Pudding

Hazelnut-Mocha Overnight Oats

Probiotic Rainbow Brekkie Bowl

Probiotic Morning Custards:
- Coconut-Matcha
- Spiced Purple Yam
- Orange Blossom–Clove

Breakfast Tabbouleh Bowl with
Avocado-Grapefruit "Hollandaise"

Calico Beet Waffles with Coconut Whip
and Tutti-Frutti Dust

Mixed Grain Pancakes with
Cardamom–Pomegranate Seed Syrup

PM

Pickled Chickpeas and Dandelion
Greens Salad

Raw Cauliflower Rice

Turmeric- and Cumin-Spiced
Cauliflower Rice

Oil and Vinegar Broccoli

Kale Salad with Sunflower Seeds, Golden
Raisins, and Lemon-Tahini Dressing

Carrot Lox

Crispy Coconut Lentils with Lime

Roasted Purple Cabbage with
Cumin and Cilantro

Beet Pastrami

Spiralized Zucchini with
Basil, Mint, and Toasted Walnuts

Creamy Batik Soup

Sweet + Sour Rainbow Radish Tacos

Bean Thread Noodle Salad with
Miso-Arugula Pesto

Kelp Noodle Japchae

Drunken Chickpea Spaghetti

Beet Falafel with Rose-Pickled Veggies

Pineapple Kimchi Summer Sunset Rolls

Avocado Pizza with Tomatillo Salsa

Broccoli-Avocado Soup

This chapter is dedicated to café food. Plates and bowls, both sweet and savory, that you'd want to eat for breakfast, brunch, or lunch, but are a little less substantial than dinner.

That includes everything from breakfast custards and multigrain pancakes to a variety of market plate-ready vegetable preps and kimchi summer rolls. Most of the sweeter dishes are reserved for a.m. consumption, while p.m. is built of savories.

But ultimately, you can really enjoy any of these at any time—that's the beauty of café food. This is the kind of food I like to eat every day—it will fill you up without weighing you down. The added bonus—it's good for you, too.

HOMEMADE CINNAMON TOAST CRUNCH

I was one of those kids—and let's be honest, teenagers—who loved cereal. Growing up, I ate cereal for breakfast; as an adult, I eat it as a snack. But in reality, cereal isn't the healthiest thing in the world you can eat since it is usually loaded with sugar and often contains artificial ingredients, too. But what about reinventing a childhood classic using ingredients that are better suited to promoting health? That's what I've done here. And the best part is that this cereal is totally addictive, just like the original. You can eat it for breakfast mixed with oats, on its own, or as a midday snack. Reach for your favorite coconut milk or the Malted Majik Milk on page 36 to mix in.

SERVES 6

6 tablespoons filtered water
2 tablespoons flax meal
1½ cups gluten-free oat flour, plus extra for working the dough
1 cup teff flour
⅓ cup plus 2 tablespoons coconut palm sugar
2 teaspoons ground cinnamon
¼ teaspoon baking powder
¼ cup coconut oil, melted
¼ cup organic unsweetened applesauce
¼ cup almond milk
2 teaspoons pure vanilla extract

1. Stir together the filtered water and flax meal in a small bowl. Let the mixture sit in the fridge to form a sticky consistency while you assemble the other ingredients.

2. Combine the oat flour, teff flour, ⅓ cup of the coconut palm sugar, 1 teaspoon of the cinnamon, and the baking powder in a medium bowl and stir to incorporate. In a small bowl, stir together the coconut oil, applesauce, almond milk, and vanilla extract to combine. Pour the coconut oil mixture into the oat flour mixture and stir until a dense, smooth dough forms. Using your hands, shape the dough into a ball. Wrap the dough in plastic wrap, transfer it to the fridge, and let it rest for 1 hour.

3. Preheat the oven to 350°F.

4. Remove the dough from the fridge. Place a large piece of parchment paper on the counter and sprinkle it with $1\frac{1}{2}$ teaspoons of the oat flour. Place the dough atop. Lay a second piece of parchment paper on top of the dough and, using a rolling pin, roll the dough between the parchment paper until it is about $\frac{1}{8}$ inch thick.

5. Combine the remaining 2 tablespoons coconut palm sugar and 1 teaspoon cinnamon in a small bowl and stir together. Sprinkle the sugar mixture atop the dough evenly to coat, and prick the dough all over with a fork. Using a pizza cutter, cut the dough into $\frac{3}{4}$-inch squares. Carefully lift the parchment paper and transfer it with the squares to a rimmed baking sheet. Bake until the squares are crunchy and light brown, about 25 minutes.

6. Let the cereal cool on the baking sheet, then gently break the squares apart and transfer them to an airtight container.

Homemade Cinnamon Toast Crunch will keep, in an airtight container at room temperature, for about 1 week.

AVO-CHIA BREKKIE PUDDING

This recipe was born by accident. I was on a mission to make really delicious avocado ice cream, and had taken out a failed batch from the freezer and left it at room temp, to the point that it had melted into the consistency of a milkshake. Instead of throwing out the almond milk–avocado–coconut nectar mix, I decided to add some chia seeds and make it into a breakfast pudding. I also tossed in dates for chew, almonds for crunch, and apple for acidity and freshness. It's delicious.

SERVES 4

1¼ cups Vanilla Bean–Almond Milk (page 28) or nut milk of choice

1 avocado, peeled and pitted

3 teaspoons coconut nectar

4 medium pitted dates, chopped

2 tablespoons chia seeds

2 tablespoons unsweetened shredded coconut, plus extra for serving

2 teaspoons flax meal

¼ cup toasted almonds (see page 161), coarsely chopped

¼ of a tart apple, such as Granny Smith, cored and cut into ¼-inch cubes

1. Combine the almond milk, avocado, and coconut nectar in a blender and blend until smooth and thick, about 30 seconds.

2. Transfer the avocado mixture to a medium bowl and add the dates, chia seeds, shredded coconut, flax meal, almonds, and apple. Stir until the chia is fully incorporated into the mixture. Cover and refrigerate until the chia seeds expand, about 20 minutes, stirring the pudding after 10 minutes to break up any chia seed clumps. The pudding should be set, but not hard; if it has become too thick, add a few more tablespoons of nut milk to loosen it.

3. Divide the pudding among four individual bowls, sprinkle with additional coconut, and serve.

Avo-Chia Brekkie Pudding will keep, in an airtight container in the refrigerator, for about 2 days (I recommend eating it sooner than later because the avocado will oxidize as it sits).

Make It Magical
Add ½ teaspoon spirulina powder to the blender along with the almond milk, avocado, and coconut nectar. Then dust a bit atop the pudding once it's done.

HAZELNUT-MOCHA OVERNIGHT OATS

Overnight oats are great because you basically combine a bunch of ingredients, then leave the mix in your fridge overnight, and in the morning breakfast is ready! You can also play around with a combination of ingredients. For example, in place of the mocha flavor profile offered here, you could mix oats, strawberries, chopped macadamia nuts, and almond milk for more of a berries-and-cream situation. Or blend oats with banana, cinnamon, and walnuts for a banana bread–esque dish. In general, I like to add chopped nuts; otherwise the milk-drenched oats are a bit one-note, texturally speaking. I also like adding coffee, as in this hazelnut-mocha version, for an extra morning boost.

SERVES 4

1 cup old-fashioned rolled oats
¼ cup toasted hazelnuts (see page 161), coarsely chopped, plus extra for serving
2 tablespoons plus 2 teaspoons tahini
1 tablespoon cacao powder, plus extra for serving
4 teaspoons pure maple syrup
¼ cup hot brewed coffee
½ teaspoon ground cardamom
½ cup Hazelnut Milk (page 33) or high-quality nut milk of your choice
½ teaspoon ground cinnamon

1. Combine the oats, hazelnuts, tahini, cacao powder, maple syrup, coffee, cardamom, hazelnut milk, and cinnamon in a large glass jar with a lid, or another airtight container, and stir to blend. Cover and refrigerate overnight.

2. In the morning, divide the overnight oats among four bowls and sprinkle with cacao powder and chopped toasted hazelnuts for garnish. Serve cold or at room temperature.

Hazelnut-Mocha Overnight Oats will keep, in an airtight container in the refrigerator, for 2 days.

Make It Magical
Add ½ teaspoon reishi, ½ teaspoon chaga, and 1 teaspoon cordyeeps to the mixture in Step 1.

PROBIOTIC RAINBOW BREKKIE BOWL

I've been thinking a lot about plant-based alternatives to yogurt. Sure, there's coconut yogurt, which I love. But coconut yogurt is not so simple to make at home because the good stuff requires cracking open fresh coconuts and letting the water and flesh mingle with probiotics for a couple of days to get that tangy fermented flavor. In considering other dishes that could stand in for yogurt, I came up with a method for making custards from different types of sweet potatoes, and then adding in probiotics (see page 17) at the end. The results are a slew of sweet potato–based probiotic custards in varying hues and flavors, like cinnamon-vanilla, coconut-matcha, and orange blossom–clove. This vibrant bowl combines all three.

SERVES 6

½ recipe Probiotic Coconut-Matcha Morning Custard (page 60)

½ recipe Probiotic Spiced Purple Yam Morning Custard (page 61)

½ recipe Probiotic Orange Blossom–Clove Morning Custard (page 62)

1 recipe Vanilla Bean–Almond Milk (page 28) or about 2½ cups high-quality nut milk of your choice

1 recipe Strawberry–Vanilla Bean Chia Jam (page 158)

Shelled pistachios, hemp seeds, crushed freeze-dried raspberries, unsweetened shredded coconut, fresh berries, assorted edible flowers, and/or sliced fresh fruit such as papaya, kiwi, dragon fruit, and figs, for garnish (the more the merrier!)

1. Place each of the three custards in a separate medium bowl and dilute with almond milk, adding 1 tablespoon at a time, until the desired pastel hue is reached.

2. Divide the orange blossom custard among six serving bowls, placing it around the outer edge of each bowl and leaving the center of the bowl empty. Spoon the coconut matcha custard into the center half of the bowl. Spoon the purple yam custard into the other side of the bowl.

3. Divide the strawberry jam among the bowls, spooning some atop the custards, and garnish the bowls as desired. Serve immediately.

PROBIOTIC COCONUT-MATCHA MORNING CUSTARD

This creamy coconut–sweet potato custard takes its green shade from finely milled green tea leaves known as matcha. Since coconut has a fairly neutral flavor, it's a great base for matcha to shine, adding a complementary hint of tropical sweetness, which enhances matcha's grassy flavor. You can find many different grades of matcha powder for sale; I always splurge on the highest grade. While I don't like judging anything based on price, with matcha it's generally safe to assume that the higher the price, the higher the quality. You generally want to spend about $30 or more for a tin of 40 grams.

SERVES 4

1 tablespoon chia seeds

4½ teaspoons filtered water

2 medium orange sweet potatoes (approximately 2½ pounds each), peeled and cut into 2-inch cubes

¾ teaspoon salt (I like pink Himalayan salt)

1 cup full-fat coconut milk

2 tablespoons raw honey

1 tablespoon coconut oil

2½ teaspoons matcha powder

1 vanilla bean, seeds scraped out (reserve the pod for another use), or 1½ teaspoons pure vanilla extract

2 teaspoons probiotic powder

¼ cup puffed rice, for garnish (optional)

2 tablespoons crushed freeze-dried strawberries, for garnish (optional)

Edible flowers, for garnish (optional)

1. Place the chia seeds in a small bowl, add the filtered water, and stir together to combine. Set aside to thicken while you prepare the sweet potatoes.

2. Meanwhile, put the sweet potatoes in a large pot, add 3 cups of tap water, ½ teaspoon of the salt, and bring to a boil over medium-high heat. Cook until the sweet potatoes are soft, about 12 minutes.

3. Remove the sweet potatoes with a slotted spoon and transfer them to the bowl of a food processor. Add the chia mixture, coconut milk, honey, coconut oil, remaining ¼ teaspoon of salt, matcha powder, and vanilla seeds and blend until smooth and custardy, about 3 minutes. Pour the custard into a large bowl, cover with plastic wrap, and chill in the fridge until cold, at least 2 hours and up to 2 days.

4. When ready to serve, stir in the probiotic powder and divide the custard among

four bowls. Garnish with the puffed rice, crushed freeze-dried strawberries, and/or edible flowers, if using.

Probiotic Coconut-Matcha Morning Custard will keep, in an airtight container in the refrigerator, for 2 days.

PROBIOTIC SPICED PURPLE YAM MORNING CUSTARD

When cooking at home, my tuber of choice is the purple yam—a deeply purple-hued root with a thick, almost chewy flesh whose flavor is reminiscent of honey. I love roasting these yams and adding them to lunch tacos (see page 88), enjoying them as a snack, or pureeing them into a sweet dessert. In this application, I use the yams as the base for a probiotic-enriched breakfast custard that's served chilled and consumed in the morning just like yogurt!

SERVES 4

1 tablespoon chia seeds

4½ teaspoons filtered water

2 medium purple yams (approximately 2½ pounds each), peeled and cut into 2-inch cubes

¾ teaspoon salt (I like pink Himalayan salt)

1 cup Vanilla Bean–Almond Milk (page 28) or high-quality nut milk of your choice

1 tablespoon coconut oil

½ teaspoon coconut palm sugar

½ teaspoon ground cinnamon

2 teaspoons probiotic powder

4 teaspoons bee pollen, for garnish (optional)

4 teaspoons spirulina crunchies, for garnish (optional)

2 tablespoons coconut flakes, for garnish (optional)

2 teaspoons cacao nibs, for garnish (optional)

1. Place the chia seeds in a small bowl, add the filtered water, and stir together to combine. Set aside to thicken while you prepare the yams.

2. Meanwhile, put the yams in a large pot, add 3 cups of tap water and ½ teaspoon of the salt, and bring to a boil over medium-high heat. Cook until the yams are soft, about 12 minutes.

3. Remove the yams with a slotted spoon and transfer them to a food processor. Add the chia mixture, almond milk, coconut oil, the remaining ¼ teaspoon of salt, coconut palm sugar, and cinnamon and blend until smooth and custardy, about 3 minutes. Pour the custard into a large bowl, cover it with plastic wrap, and chill in the fridge until cold, at least 2 hours and up to 2 days.

4. When ready to serve, stir in the probiotic powder and divide the custard among four bowls. Garnish with the bee pollen, spirulina crunchies, coconut flakes, and/or cacao nibs, if desired.

Probiotic Spiced Purple Yam Morning Custard will keep, in an airtight container in the refrigerator, for 2 days.

PROBIOTIC ORANGE BLOSSOM–CLOVE MORNING CUSTARD

Foods flavored with flowers, such as rose, lavender, and orange blossom, tend to elicit love or hate responses. While some believe these ingredients taste soapy or perfumey, I am personally a big fan, especially of orange blossom for its pretty, exotic taste. Here, the orange blossom flavor comes from both the honey made from the flower's pollen and the orange blossom water.

Orange blossom honey is pretty common, but if you can't find it, feel free to sub in another type of honey and add an extra splash of the flower water.

SERVES 4

1 tablespoon chia seeds

4½ teaspoons filtered water

2 medium orange sweet potatoes (about 2½ pounds each), peeled and cut into 2-inch cubes

1 cup Vanilla Bean–Almond Milk, (page 28) or high-quality nut milk of your choice

4 teaspoons orange blossom honey

2 teaspoons food-grade orange blossom water (see Note)

1 teaspoon ground cloves

¾ teaspoon salt (I like pink Himalayan salt)

2 teaspoons probiotic powder

Matcha-dusted hemp seeds (see page 22), for garnish (optional)

1. Place the chia seeds in a small bowl, add the filtered water, and stir together to combine. Set aside to thicken while you prepare the sweet potatoes.

2. Meanwhile, put the sweet potatoes in a large pot, add 3 cups of tap water and ½ teaspoon of the salt, and bring to a boil over medium-high heat. Cook until the sweet potatoes are soft, about 12 minutes.

3. Remove the sweet potatoes with a slotted spoon and transfer them to the bowl of a food processor.

Add the chia mixture, almond milk, honey, orange blossom water, cloves, and remaining ¼ teaspoon of salt and blend until smooth and custardy, about 3 minutes. Pour the custard into a large bowl, cover with plastic wrap, and chill in the fridge until cold, at least 2 hours and up to 2 days.

4. When ready to serve, stir in the probiotic powder and divide the custard among four bowls. Garnish with the matcha-dusted hemp seeds, if using.

Probiotic Orange Blossom–Clove Morning Custard will keep, in an airtight container in the refrigerator, for 2 days.

Note: Food-grade orange blossom water, also called orange flower water, is made by macerating bitter orange blossoms in water, and then distilling that liquid. It's a popular ingredient in Middle Eastern cooking and should be used in moderation because it can have a powerfully floral flavor. Orange blossom water is sold at Middle Eastern markets, some grocery stores, and online.

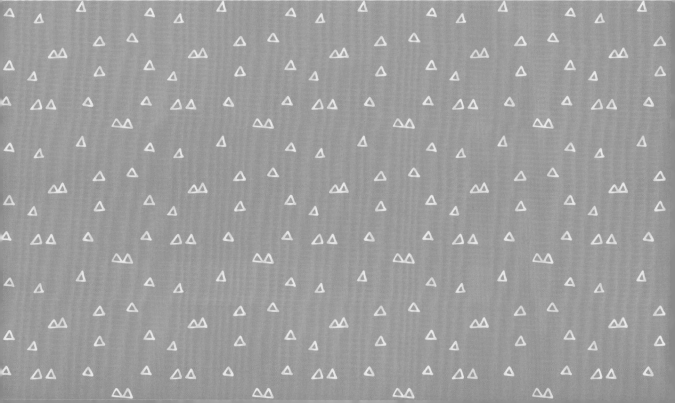

Carrot Lox

Avocado-
Grapefruit
"Hollandaise"

Coconut Whip

Tutti-Frutti Dust

Cardamom–Pomegranate
Seed Syrup

Mixed Grain Pancakes

Breakfast Tabbouleh

Calico Beet Waffles

BREAKFAST TABBOULEH BOWL WITH AVOCADO-GRAPEFRUIT "HOLLANDAISE"

I like the idea of a breakfast salad. So many breakfast bowls start with grain as a base, but what about simply focusing on veggies? Here, I've taken tabbouleh—traditionally made with bulgur wheat—and I've subbed in cauliflower rice. As a dressing, in place of the typical lemon and olive oil, I've added a reworked take on the classic hollandaise sauce, which is made with avocado for creamy richness.

Combine the cauliflower rice, parsley, cucumber, tomato, scallion, garlic, salt, pepper, lemon juice, olive oil, and dill in a medium bowl and toss together. Divide the tabbouleh among four bowls. Add about 1 tablespoon of the "hollandaise" (or more or less to taste) and a few slices of carrot lox to each bowl. Serve immediately.

Breakfast Tabbouleh Bowl with Avocado-Grapefruit "Hollandaise" will keep, in separate airtight containers in the refrigerator, for 1 day.

SERVES 4

1 cup Raw Cauliflower Rice (page 76)

1 cup chopped fresh flat-leaf (Italian) parsley leaves

1 cup diced cucumber

1 cup diced tomato

2 tablespoons finely sliced scallion

1 teaspoon minced garlic

1 teaspoon fine sea salt

¼ teaspoon freshly ground black pepper

3 tablespoons fresh lemon juice

1 tablespoon olive oil

2 tablespoons chopped fresh dill

Avocado-Grapefruit "Hollandaise" (page 170)

Carrot Lox (page 80), for serving

CALICO BEET WAFFLES WITH COCONUT WHIP AND TUTTI-FRUTTI DUST

These dark pink tie-dye waffles get their vibrant color from beets, which are rich in antioxidants and channel a sweet, earthy flavor. Chinese five-spice powder—a fragrant mix made from a combination of cinnamon, star anise, fennel, Sichuan pepper, and cloves—adds a subtly exotic taste to the beet batter, and both of those flavors pair well with the strawberry dust that's sprinkled atop.

When making these waffles, I like to leave the outer inch or so of the waffle iron empty, only filling the center—when you close the iron, the batter spills out asymmetrically, creating a lacy, organic shape.

SERVES 3

2 cups brown rice flour

2 Chia Eggs (page 12)

2 cups Hazelnut Milk (page 33) or other high-quality nut milk of your choice

¼ heaping cup Beet Puree (recipe follows)

2 tablespoons coconut oil, melted, plus extra for greasing the waffle iron

2 tablespoons coconut palm sugar

2 teaspoons Chinese five-spice powder

2 teaspoons pure vanilla extract

1 teaspoon baking powder

¼ teaspoon salt (I like pink Himalayan salt)

Coconut Whip (page 169), for serving

2 tablespoons Tutti-Frutti Dust (page 170), for garnish

1. Combine 1 cup of the rice flour, 1 chia egg, 1 cup of the hazelnut milk, 4 tablespoons of the beet puree, 1 tablespoon of the coconut oil, 1 tablespoon of the coconut palm sugar, the Chinese five-spice powder, 1 teaspoon of the vanilla, ½ teaspoon of the baking powder, and ⅛ teaspoon of the salt in a medium bowl and whisk to blend into a dark pink batter.

2. In a second medium bowl, combine the remaining 1 cup rice flour, 1 chia egg, 1 cup hazelnut milk, 1½ teaspoons beet puree, 1 tablespoon coconut oil, 1 tablespoon coconut palm sugar, 1 teaspoon vanilla, ½ teaspoon baking powder, and ⅛ teaspoon salt and whisk to blend into a light pink batter.

3. Grease the waffle iron on top and bottom with coconut oil and heat the iron according to the manufacturer's directions.

4. Ladle about ¼ cup or more of the dark pink batter onto the waffle iron, dropping small amounts haphazardly into the center of the iron and leaving some gaps in between. Fill in the gaps with about ¼ cup or more of the light pink batter (leave the outer inch or so of the waffle iron bare) so you have an organically shaped circle of batter in the center of the iron. Close the iron and cook the waffle until light brown and crisp on the outside, about 9 minutes, depending on your waffle iron.

5. Carefully remove the waffle from the iron, transfer it to a plate, and cover with aluminum foil to keep warm. Repeat with the remaining batters (it should make 3 waffles).

6. Serve the waffles warm, topping each with 2 tablespoons of coconut whip and a sprinkling of the tutti-frutti dust.

BEET PUREE

1. Fill a medium pot halfway with tap water and add the beet. Bring to a boil over medium-high heat, then lower the heat to medium and simmer until the beet is soft when pierced with a fork, about 30 minutes. Remove the beet from the water with a slotted spoon and set aside to cool to room temperature.

2. Using your hands, slip the skin off the cooled beet (it will come off easily). Transfer the beet to a food processor and blend until the beet is pureed, about 20 seconds. If needed, add water, a teaspoon at a time, until a puree forms.

Beet Puree will keep, covered in the refrigerator, for up to 5 days.

MAKES ABOUT ⅓ CUP
1 medium red beet, unpeeled and scrubbed

MIXED GRAIN PANCAKES WITH CARDAMOM–POMEGRANATE SEED SYRUP

When I lived in Venice, California, my go-to weekend brunch spot was a place on Abbot Kinney named Axe. I am heartbroken that Axe is now closed, but the memory of the Cali-Japanese–inspired café lives on through this pancake. Axe was famous for its nine-grain pancake, a single, inch-thick number that filled an entire entrée-size plate and came crowned with a matchbox-size cut of butter and some maple syrup. As someone who was entirely obsessed with Axe's pancake, and couldn't visit the place without ordering it, this version comes very close, even without animal ingredients or gluten. Note, you'll have to precook the grains and then incorporate them into the batter. It's also a great way to repurpose any leftover grains you might have on hand!

SERVES 3

4½ teaspoons filtered water

1 tablespoon chia seeds

⅔ cup cooked millet

⅔ cup cooked white quinoa

⅔ cup amaranth flour

⅓ cup gluten-free all-purpose flour

⅓ cup brown rice flour

⅔ cup coconut palm sugar

¼ cup whole flaxseeds

2 tablespoons poppy seeds

2 tablespoons psyllium husks

1 teaspoon baking powder

½ teaspoon salt (I like pink Himalayan salt)

¼ teaspoon baking soda

1 cup high-quality almond milk, preferably homemade (see page 28)

About ½ cup coconut oil, melted

2 teaspoons pure vanilla extract

3 tablespoons pure maple syrup

1 teaspoon ground cardamom

⅔ cup fresh pomegranate seeds

¼ cup coconut cream (see page 9), for serving

3 tablespoons raw or roasted shelled pistachios, coarsely chopped, for garnish

1. Combine the filtered water and chia seeds in a small bowl and stir together to mix. Set aside in the fridge to thicken while you make the batter.

2. Place the millet, quinoa, amaranth flour, gluten-free all-purpose flour, rice flour, coconut palm sugar, flaxseeds, poppy seeds, psyllium husks, baking powder, salt, and baking soda in a large bowl and stir together to combine.

3. Stir together the almond milk, 3 tablespoons of the melted coconut oil, the vanilla, and the reserved chia mixture in a medium bowl. Pour the almond milk mixture into the millet mixture and stir together to form a thick batter.

4. Stir together the maple syrup, cardamom, and pomegranate seeds in a small bowl to combine; set aside.

5. Warm 1 tablespoon of the coconut oil in a small frying pan over medium heat. Add one third of the batter and, using the back of a spoon, press it into a circle about ¾ inch thick and 5 to 6 inches in diameter. Cook until the pancake is light brown on the bottom and set on top, about 4 minutes. Using a large spatula, carefully flip the pancake, adding a little bit more coconut oil to the pan if needed. Cook until the pancake is light brown, 3 minutes more. Using the spatula, carefully transfer the pancake to a large plate and cover it with aluminum foil to keep warm. Repeat with the remaining batter, adding more coconut oil to the pan each time.

6. Place each pancake on a plate and spread the coconut cream on top. Spoon some of the pomegranate seeds and maple-cardamom syrup over the cream, and sprinkle with the pistachios. Serve immediately.

PICKLED CHICKPEAS AND DANDELION GREENS SALAD

E at your . . . weeds? You probably don't really think about eating those yellow flowers that might grow in your front yard, or the green leaves attached. However, dandelions are entirely edible—you can eat the greens raw in a salad, or even sautéed. They're generally for sale in the spring at farmers' markets, and add a bitter vegetal flavor to dishes. Look for the young leaves, which are less aggressively bitter than the larger, older ones. And if you're unable to find dandelion greens, you could sub in other bitter leaves like radicchio.

This salad mixes pickled chickpeas with a spicy mustard vinaigrette that tempers the sharpness of the greens. I've added beets to the pickling brine for fun, which tints the chickpeas a pale pink hue. You can, of course, omit this step. The longer you pickle the chickpeas, the more magenta they will become. For a super-bright pink, pickle them overnight. And in the morning when you strain the pickling brine, hang onto it and then use it to pickle sliced white onions, and dye them bright pink, too!

SERVES 4

For the Pickled Chickpeas

1 cup apple cider vinegar

2 tablespoons plus 1½ teaspoons raw honey

4½ teaspoons fine sea salt

1 small raw red beet, unpeeled and scrubbed (optional but recommended)

2 cups cooked chickpeas

For the Vinaigrette and Salad

¼ cup Dijon mustard

¼ cup vegetable oil

2 tablespoons apple cider vinegar

2 tablespoons raw honey

½ teaspoon fine sea salt

¼ teaspoon freshly ground black pepper

¼ small shallot, chopped

¼ teaspoon grated fresh ginger

2 tablespoons filtered water

6 cups dandelion greens or other bitter greens

Seeded Togarashi (see page 172)

Edible flowers, for garnish (optional)

1. Make the pickled chickpeas: Combine the apple cider vinegar, honey, salt, and beet, if using, in a medium pot and bring to a boil over medium-high heat. Remove from the heat and let cool to room temperature.

2. Place the chickpeas in a medium bowl and add the cooled pickle brine. Let sit at room temperature for 3 hours, or covered in the refrigerator overnight. Strain the chickpeas from the brine (save the brine for another use, if you like).

3. Make the vinaigrette: Combine the mustard, oil, apple cider vinegar, honey, salt, pepper, shallot, ginger, and filtered water in a blender or food processor and blend until the dressing looks creamy and white, about 1 minute. Set aside.

4. Place the dandelion greens in a large bowl, add the dressing to taste, and toss to coat the greens. Add the chickpeas and toss again.

5. Divide the salad among four plates and sprinkle the togarashi atop each. Garnish with edible flowers, if using. Serve immediately.

Rainbow Cauliflower Rice

Beet Pastrami

Crispy Coconut Lentils with Lime

Roasted Purple Cabbage with Cumin and Cilantro

Kale Salad with Sunflower Seeds, Golden Raisins, and Lemon-Tahini Dressing

Spiralized Zucchini with Basil, Mint, and Toasted Walnuts

Oil and Vinegar Broccoli

Carrot Lox

RAW CAULIFLOWER RICE

Cauliflower rice is kind of amazing. Just like regular rice, it is a blank slate to which you can add a bevy of flavors. However, where cauliflower rice has an edge over regular rice is that it's far lower in calories and carbs and it's naturally rich in fiber and vitamins. Also, unlike regular rice, it can be consumed both raw and cooked (see Variations).

While places like Trader Joe's now sell frozen and refrigerated cauliflower rice, it's a cinch to make your own—all you need is cauliflower and a food processor or box grater. I love to add cauliflower rice—raw or cooked—to tacos and salad, or simply eat it on its own as a side. Oh, and when in season, I mix white cauliflower with purple and Romanesco, the pretty green kind you'll find at farmers' markets during the summer, which makes for a colorful medley (see Rainbow Cauliflower Rice).

MAKES ABOUT 4 CUPS

1 head (about 2 pounds) cauliflower (I like to use a mix of colors whenever possible)

....

Wash and dry the cauliflower. Pull off and discard the outer leaves and cut the head into 4 quarters. If using a box grater, position it over a large bowl and grate the cauliflower to the size of rice. Alternatively, divide the quarters into florets, place half of them in the bowl of the food processor, and process until the cauliflower is the size of rice, about 20 seconds, then transfer to a large bowl; repeat with the remaining cauliflower.

Raw Cauliflower Rice will keep, in an airtight container in the refrigerator, for 2 days, or in the freezer for about 3 months. Thaw before using.

Variations
Cooked Cauliflower Rice:
Heat ½ cup olive oil in a large pan over medium-high heat, add the cauliflower rice and

salt and pepper to taste and cook, stirring frequently, until the cauliflower is tender and loses some opacity, about 8 minutes.

Rainbow Cauliflower Rice: If you're going to mix different colors of cauliflower, use equal portions of each, then proceed with the recipes to make raw or cooked cauliflower rice.

TURMERIC- AND CUMIN-SPICED CAULIFLOWER RICE

This earthy yellow rice channels Indian cooking thanks to the addition of turmeric and cumin. The flavor is exotic but not overpowering, and you can eat this rice on its own, tossed with salad, wrapped into a breakfast burrito (a personal favorite), or many of the other ways you'd typically consume rice.

....

Heat a large pan over medium-high heat and add the olive oil. When the oil is hot, add the cauliflower, cumin, 1½ teaspoons of salt, coriander, turmeric, and pepper and stir to combine. Cook, stirring frequently, until the cauliflower is cooked through and tender, about 8 minutes. Stir in the lemon juice, season to taste with additional salt and black pepper, and serve hot.

Turmeric- and Cumin-Spiced Cauliflower Rice will keep, in an airtight container in the refrigerator, for 2 days. Reheat leftover rice before serving.

SERVES 4 TO 6
½ cup olive oil
4 cups Raw Cauliflower Rice (page 76)
5 teaspoons ground cumin
1½ teaspoons fine sea salt, plus extra as needed
1 teaspoon ground coriander
1 teaspoon ground turmeric
½ teaspoon freshly ground black pepper, plus extra as needed
2 tablespoons fresh lemon juice

OIL AND VINEGAR BROCCOLI

B y now I've probably made versions of this recipe close to one hundred times. I've topped this broccoli with Parmesan cheese, squeezed lemon atop, and mixed in toasted almonds—sometimes separately, sometimes all at once. The dish is especially addictive because as the broccoli roasts in the oven, it gets crisp and a bit caramelized from the oil in which it's tossed. I love this recipe because it's easy, and can be served warm or cold. Which means you can prep it several hours before your dinner party (or just dinner) and have it ready to go. If you have leftovers, throw the broccoli into a salad or mix it with cooked quinoa the next day.

SERVES 4

1 large head broccoli, trimmed and cut into florets with stems attached

6 tablespoons olive oil

1 teaspoon fine sea salt, plus extra as needed

½ teaspoon freshly ground black pepper, plus extra as needed

1 tablespoon apple cider vinegar

1 teaspoon minced fresh garlic

½ teaspoon crushed red pepper flakes

1. Preheat the oven to 450°F.

2. Toss together the broccoli, olive oil, salt, and black pepper on a rimmed baking sheet. Roast, tossing occasionally, until tender and golden brown, about 25 minutes.

3. Drizzle the vinegar evenly over the hot broccoli, sprinkle it with the minced garlic and red pepper flakes, and toss on the baking sheet to coat. Season to taste with more salt and black pepper. Serve warm or cold.

Oil and Vinegar Broccoli will keep, in an airtight container in the refrigerator, for up to 2 days.

KALE SALAD WITH SUNFLOWER SEEDS, GOLDEN RAISINS, AND LEMON-TAHINI DRESSING

Despite the ubiquity of kale salads, I love the leaf nonetheless, and I often find myself craving it while on the road for long stretches of time. My ideal salad is always made from a base of kale. Here you'll find subtle umami from the crunchy sunflower seeds and tahini, balanced by the occasional sweetness from golden raisins.

Pro tip: Make this salad several hours before you plan to eat it. The kale is a sturdy-leafed green, and the acidity in the lemon juice helps soften it while it sits. The recipe calls for removing the tough stems from the leaves, but fear not—you can save them for use in another dish (see page 108).

Place the shredded kale in a large bowl. Combine the olive oil, tahini, lemon juice, salt, honey, and soy sauce in a small bowl and whisk to emulsify. Drizzle the dressing over the kale and use your hands to massage it into the leaves so that the dressing is evenly distributed. Sprinkle the sunflower seeds and golden raisins atop and toss lightly. Cover and refrigerate for a few hours before serving.

Kale Salad with Sunflower Seeds, Golden Raisins, and Lemon-Tahini Dressing will keep, in an airtight container in the refrigerator, overnight.

SERVES 4

About ¾ bunch lacinato kale, stems removed (reserve them for another use) and leaves shredded (to equal 4 cups softly packed, shredded leaves)

3 tablespoons olive oil

1 tablespoon plus 1 teaspoon tahini (sesame paste)

1 tablespoon fresh lemon juice

¼ teaspoon fine sea salt

¼ teaspoon raw honey

¼ teaspoon gluten-free soy sauce

⅓ cup roasted, unsalted sunflower seeds

¼ cup golden raisins

CARROT LOX

It wasn't until recently that I started liking lox. Growing up, many of my friends customarily ate those slices of cured, smoked salmon atop bagels swiped with cream cheese, but it wasn't really my thing. Have you heard that your taste buds change every seven years? Somewhere along the line, in the last few years, I started enjoying the salty, fishy flavor of lox. In considering a plant-based alternative to mimic that aquatic taste, I've brined carrot slices in a spicy and acidic nori marinade. This process takes a few days, but the prep is quick and easy and then you just let the carrots hang out. And while their texture isn't *quite* the same as lox—more like a slippery, softer, but still al dente, carrot slice—I'm still loving the result. This carrot lox is super versatile, and can be added to a breakfast or lunch bowl, or layered atop toast.

SERVES 8

4 large carrots, trimmed and peeled
1 sheet toasted nori
2 tablespoons plus 1 teaspoon rice vinegar
¼ cup gluten-free soy sauce
4½ teaspoons olive oil
1½ teaspoons chopped fresh dill
½ teaspoon chipotle powder
½ teaspoon fresh lemon juice
¼ teaspoon fine sea salt
¼ teaspoon freshly ground black pepper

1. Preheat the oven to 350°F.

2. Using a mandoline (or a carrot peeler), shave the carrots lengthwise into strips about $\frac{1}{16}$ inch thick. Transfer the carrot shavings to a piece of aluminum foil, arranging them in a single layer (more or less) on one half and then folding the other half over and crimping the edges to make a packet.

Place the carrot packet in the oven and roast until the carrots are tender, but not falling apart, about 1 hour. Transfer the carrot packet to the fridge and chill for 1 hour.

3. Meanwhile, combine the nori, rice vinegar, soy sauce, olive oil, dill, chipotle powder, lemon juice, salt, and black pepper in a blender or food

processor and blend until everything is incorporated and the nori is broken down, about 2 minutes.

4. Remove the carrots from the fridge and transfer the slices to a medium bowl. Add the marinade and stir so that the carrots are completely coated. Arrange the carrots on a flat serving dish so they overlap partially like shingles; pour the remaining marinade on top. Cover with plastic wrap and chill in the fridge for 3 days (or up to 5) before serving.

Carrot Lox will keep, in an airtight container with its marinade, in the refrigerator for up to 2 days.

CRISPY COCONUT LENTILS WITH LIME

This is one of my favorite recipes in the book. Think crispy lentils with a subtle coconut flavor and bright notes of lime, plus a savoriness from the Pastrami Spice Blend—this dish bursts with flavor. I love to eat these lentils on their own, built into a veggie bowl, or even as a garnish on other dishes. They're absolutely addictive!

SERVES 4

2 teaspoons fine sea salt

2 cups black lentils, rinsed and picked over to remove any debris

¼ cup coconut oil

4 teaspoons Pastrami Spice (page 173)

¼ cup fresh lime juice

2 teaspoons freshly grated lime zest

¼ teaspoon freshly ground black pepper

1. Preheat the oven to 450°F.

2. Heat 4 cups of tap water in a large pot over medium-high heat, add 1 teaspoon of the salt, and bring to a boil. Add the lentils, reduce the heat to medium, and simmer until the water has almost completely evaporated and the lentils have softened and are about 90 percent cooked but still al dente, about 20 minutes. Stir in the coconut oil.

3. Spoon the lentils onto a rimmed baking sheet and smooth them out into a

single even layer. Roast, stirring every 10 minutes, until the lentils are crispy, about 30 minutes.

4. Transfer the lentils to a medium bowl and stir in the Pastrami Spice blend, lime juice, lime zest,

pepper, and remaining 1 teaspoon of salt. Serve hot.

Crispy Coconut Lentils with Lime will keep, in an airtight container in the refrigerator, for 2 days.

ROASTED PURPLE CABBAGE WITH CUMIN AND CILANTRO

Channeling a Middle Eastern flavor profile thanks to the trifecta of cumin, pomegranate molasses, and cilantro, this tasty cabbage has spice, freshness, and acidity. One of my favorite things about cooking with naturally purple foods is that when you introduce an acid, like lemon juice, the purple turns to pink. So if you serve this cabbage on a plate, when you squeeze fresh lemon juice atop, the cabbage will sport a cool pink-purple tie-dye look.

A couple of notes on this recipe. If you don't like spice in your food, leave out the cayenne. If you can't find pomegranate molasses (which is really delicious, I should add), then you can leave it out and just make a dressing from lemon and garlic.

SERVES 5
1 medium head purple cabbage
5 tablespoons olive oil, plus extra as needed
2 teaspoons ground cumin
1⅛ teaspoon cayenne pepper
⅓ cup fresh lemon juice, or more to taste
2½ teaspoons pomegranate molasses (see Note)
3 garlic cloves, minced
¼ cup fresh cilantro leaves, chopped
2 teaspoons freshly grated lemon zest
Coarse sea salt

1. Preheat the oven to 400°F. Line a rimmed baking sheet with parchment paper.

2. Slice the cabbage through the core, cutting from top to bottom into 5 slabs each about 1 inch thick (save the two rounded outer slices for another use). Arrange the cabbage slabs on the prepared baking sheet and drizzle each slice with about 1 tablespoon of the olive oil, flipping each piece over to coat both sides.

3. Stir together the cumin and cayenne in a small bowl. Sprinkle the spice blend evenly over the cabbage slices, using your fingers to massage the oil and spices into the cabbage segments. If the cabbage looks dry, add another teaspoon or so of olive oil to coat it.

4. Bake until the cabbage slices are tender when pierced with a fork, about 30 minutes.

5. Meanwhile, put the lemon juice, pomegranate molasses, and garlic in a small bowl and stir to combine.

6. Remove the cabbage slices from the oven and transfer them to a serving platter. Drizzle the lemon juice mixture evenly over the cabbage slices, sprinkle them with the cilantro and lemon zest, and season to taste with salt. Serve immediately.

Roasted Purple Cabbage with Cumin and Cilantro will keep, in an airtight container in the refrigerator, for 2 days. Reheat leftovers in the oven.

Note: Pomegranate molasses is sold at some grocery stores, Middle Eastern markets, and online at Amazon.com.

BEET PASTRAMI

This recipe is inspired by the typical spice blend that coats the outside of pastrami, giving the meat its signature savory flavor. Here, rather than rubbing the blend into beef, you're using it to coat beets. I like to take these beet slices and layer them on avocado toast, add them to salads, or use them to build a market plate. Note, the pastrami spice mix recipe makes more than is needed to coat the beets. Store the leftover spice blend in a glass jar and sprinkle it directly atop your favorite dip or use it to spice up roasted veggies.

MAKES ENOUGH FOR ABOUT 20 TOASTS; SERVES ABOUT 10

1 teaspoon mustard seeds
1 teaspoon coriander seeds
1 tablespoon coconut palm sugar
1 tablespoon garlic powder
1 tablespoon onion powder
1 teaspoon garam masala
1 teaspoon freshly ground black pepper
2 large cooked beets, trimmed and peeled (see page 68)

1. Using a mortar and pestle or a food processor, blend the spices until they are coarsely ground and combined (they should not be completely broken down into a fine dust).

2. Preheat the oven to 350°F. Line a rimmed baking sheet with parchment paper.

3. Using a mandoline (or a sharp chef's knife), slice the beets into thin rounds about ⅛ inch thick. Arrange the beet slices on the prepared baking sheet so that the slices overlap one another halfway, like shingles. Sprinkle 4 teaspoons of the pastrami spice blend liberally atop the beets (store the leftover spice blend in a glass jar; it will keep in an airtight container at room temperature for 6 months).

4. Bake until the beet slices look dry and shriveled (they will be chewy like fruit leather), about 30 minutes. Let the beet slices cool on the baking sheet before using.

Beet Pastrami will keep, in an airtight container in the refrigerator, for up to 3 days.

SPIRALIZED ZUCCHINI WITH BASIL, MINT, AND TOASTED WALNUTS

For me, summers are synonymous with basil pesto pasta—a dish my father would make without fail every June through August, thanks to the abundance of spicy basil leaves available out east on Long Island. My mother grows five types of basil at our summer home, so sometimes the pesto would be flavored traditionally Italian, while other times Thai basil would offer a twist. Regardless of the type, to me, basil equals summer, which equals good times. In an effort to offer up a cleaner riff on pesto pasta, I've subbed in zucchini spirals for spaghetti, and added a bit of mint for extra freshness. If you don't have a spiralizer at home (they're available online for about $30), you can use a carrot peeler to shave zucchini into wide ribbons.

SERVES 4

2 medium-large zucchini (to make about 2 cups of spirals)

1 cup packed thinly sliced fresh basil leaves

½ cup packed thinly sliced fresh mint leaves

2 tablespoons plus 1½ teaspoons extra-virgin olive oil

2 tablespoons fresh lemon juice

2 teaspoons minced fresh garlic

½ teaspoon crushed red pepper flakes

½ teaspoon fine sea salt

¼ teaspoon freshly ground black pepper

½ cup toasted walnuts (see page 161), coarsely chopped

1. Using a spiralizer, spiralize the zucchini into spaghetti-like strands (alternatively, use a carrot peeler to shave the zucchini into long, thin strips). Place the strands in a large bowl, add the basil and mint leaves, and toss to incorporate.

2. Combine the olive oil, lemon juice, garlic, red pepper flakes, salt, and black pepper in a small bowl and whisk briefly to emulsify.

3. Pour the dressing over the zucchini mixture and toss to distribute it evenly. Sprinkle the toasted walnuts atop, mix, and serve.

Spiralized Zucchini with Basil, Mint, and Toasted Walnuts will keep, in an airtight container in the refrigerator, for 2 days. Bring to room temperature before serving.

CREAMY BATIK SOUP

This vibrant soup—named after the colorful Indonesian fabric it resembles—is perfect for summer because it can be eaten warm or at room temperature, and its creaminess comes from protein-rich chia seeds instead of heavy carbs like rice or potatoes. Thanks to the miso, sesame oil, and rice vinegar, it takes on an Asian flavor, thus transforming cabbage, which can taste rather bland, into a bright, umami-rich meal. For the soup's garnish, I like to squeeze lime atop, which adds acidity and stains the surface a fun pink hue. Then I sprinkle on togarashi, also known as shichimi togarashi, a common Japanese spice blend made from seven ingredients.

SERVES 4

3 tablespoons fresh lime juice

2 tablespoons chia seeds

4 cups plus 3 tablespoons filtered water

4 cups chopped purple cabbage

4 garlic cloves, peeled

2 shallots, peeled

½ teaspoon fine sea salt

¼ teaspoon freshly ground black pepper

4 teaspoons white miso paste (see page 15)

2 teaspoons raw honey

2 tablespoons rice wine vinegar

2 tablespoons olive oil

1 teaspoon toasted sesame oil

Seeded Togarashi (see page 172) or store-bought (see Note), for garnish

Freshly grated orange and/or lime zest, for garnish

Lime wedges, for serving

1. Place the lime juice, chia seeds, and 3 tablespoons of the filtered water in a small bowl and stir together to combine. Set aside to thicken while you assemble the soup.

2. Heat the remaining 4 cups of filtered water in a large pot over medium-high heat. Add the cabbage, garlic, shallots, salt, and pepper. Lower the heat to medium and simmer, uncovered, until the cabbage is tender, about 20 minutes.

3. Carefully transfer the cabbage, garlic, shallots, and simmering liquid to a blender or food processor. Add the miso paste, honey, rice wine vinegar, olive oil, and sesame oil and puree until the mixture is smooth and velvety, about 3 minutes.

4. Divide the soup among four bowls and spoon one-quarter of the chia seed mixture into the center of each bowl. Garnish with togarashi, lime zest, and orange zest.

Creamy Batik Soup will keep, in an airtight container in the refrigerator, for 2 days.

Note: If you don't want to make your own togarashi, you can buy it in Asian food stores, at Whole Foods, and online at Amazon.com.

SWEET + SOUR RAINBOW RADISH TACOS

F or a light yet still satisfying take on tacos, this colorful version replaces the traditional corn tortillas with large, thinly sliced radishes. Inside you'll find a bit of creamy tahini, wedges of baked sweet potato, kimchi for acidity, and a hit of togarashi for nutty spice. Try these petite tacos for breakfast, lunch, or a midday snack.

....

1. Preheat the oven to 350°F.

2. Prick the sweet potato all over with a fork and place it on a baking sheet. Bake until soft, about 25 minutes. Transfer the sweet potato to a cutting board and carefully slice it lengthwise into 8 long wedges. Sprinkle the wedges with the salt, cayenne, and black pepper.

3. Meanwhile, fill a large bowl with tap water and add a cup of ice. Using a chef's knife or mandoline, slice the radish into very thin rounds, each about $\frac{1}{16}$ inch thick. Stack the slices into two stacks, mold them into a taco shape, then tie them in place with butcher's twine (or unwaxed, unflavored dental floss in a pinch). Submerge them in the ice bath to firm up (this will help them hold their shape), at least 10 minutes or up to an hour.

4. When the sweet potato wedges are ready, remove the radish taco shells from the ice bath, snip off

the string, and pat them dry with a paper towel. Assemble the tacos one by one: Smear ½ teaspoon of the tahini in the center of each taco shell, and sprinkle 4½ teaspoons of the cauliflower rice on top. Layer on 1 sweet potato wedge and 1 avocado wedge, then top with 1 tablespoon of the kimchi and sprinkle with ½ teaspoon of the togarashi.

5. Serve the tacos immediately, a few to a plate, garnished with lime wedges.

Notes: I like to make the rice with purple cauliflower or a combination of green Romanesco and white and purple cauliflowers to amp up the rainbow effect. Feel free to make it ahead of time and reheat it in a small pan over medium heat or in the microwave.

Kimchi, a staple in Korean cooking, is a salty-sour fermented vegetable dish. It's available in the Asian foods aisle at most supermarkets.

MAKES 8 SMALL TACOS

1 orange sweet potato, (about 4 inches long), unpeeled and scrubbed
¼ teaspoon fine sea salt
¼ teaspoon cayenne pepper
⅛ teaspoon freshly ground black pepper
1 large black radish, 3 to 4 inches in diameter, scrubbed and unpeeled
4 teaspoons tahini (sesame paste)
¾ cup warm Turmeric- and Cumin-Spiced Cauliflower Rice (page 77; see Notes)
1 avocado, peeled, pitted, and sliced lengthwise into 8 wedges
8 tablespoons kimchi (see Notes)
4 teaspoons Seeded Togarashi, (page 172) or store-bought
Lime wedges, for garnish

BEAN THREAD NOODLE SALAD WITH MISO-ARUGULA PESTO

This recipe was born by accident. I had set out to make a vegan arugula-basil pesto, and, midway through, I decided that the sauce was lacking the salty umami traditionally added by an aged cheese like Parmesan or Pecorino Romano. I paused for a moment, thinking about nonanimal ingredients that could add a similar flavor, and miso paste popped into my mind. Miso and shiso, sometimes described as "Japanese basil," are a happy match, and as it turns out, Italian basil and miso play nicely, too. You want your pesto to err slightly on the salty side because you'll be tossing it with noodles and also a decent amount of fresh arugula leaves.

Personally, I love the slippery, chewy texture of bean thread noodles in this dish, but if you can't find them, try subbing in sweet potato noodles, or even soba (if you're avoiding gluten, just make sure that your soba is made from 100 percent buckwheat and not the more common 80:20 buckwheat-wheat mix). While this recipe makes three entrée-size portions, if you want to make this for a larger group, just double the measurements!

SERVES 3

1 package (about 2 ounces) dried bean thread noodles

¼ cup plus 2 tablespoons pine nuts, toasted (see page 161)

1 tablespoon nutritional yeast (see Note)

4 cups packed fresh baby arugula leaves

1½ cups packed fresh basil leaves

4½ teaspoons red miso paste

1 tablespoon extra-virgin olive oil

1 garlic clove, peeled

¼ teaspoon fine sea salt, plus extra as needed

Freshly ground black pepper

Juice of 1 lemon

1. Fill a medium pot halfway with tap water and bring to a boil over high heat. Remove the pot from the heat and add the bean thread noodles. Let the noodles steep, stirring occasionally, until they're soft and chewy, about 20 minutes. Drain the noodles in a colander and set them aside.

2. Combine ¼ cup of the pine nuts, the nutritional yeast, 2 cups of the arugula leaves, the basil leaves, miso paste, olive oil, garlic, and the ¼ teaspoon salt in a food processor and blend until everything is incorporated and the sauce looks creamy and green, about 90 seconds. Scrape down the side of the bowl with a spatula and blend again for another 20 seconds.

3. Meanwhile, roughly chop the remaining 2 tablespoons of pine nuts. Transfer the noodles to a large bowl and add the remaining 2 cups of arugula leaves. Pour the pesto over all, tossing with tongs so the pesto is evenly distributed between the noodles and arugula.

Season to taste with salt and pepper.

4. Just before serving, sprinkle the chopped pine nuts on the noodles and squeeze lemon juice atop. Toss again and serve warm or at room temperature.

Bean Thread Noodle Salad with Miso-Arugula Pesto will keep, in an airtight container in the refrigerator, for up to 2 days.

Note: Nutritional yeast, which comes in small, delicate yellow flakes, is a type of deactivated (i.e., dead) yeast that lends dishes a nutty, cheesy, umami-rich flavor. It's commonly sprinkled atop salads and adds a savory flavor to sauces (it's also surprisingly delicious on popcorn).

KELP NOODLE JAPCHAE

I grew up eating a ton of Asian food, mainly because it's what my father loves. Whenever my family would go out for Korean food, my requisite dish was always *japchae*, a dish made from chewy, slippery sweet potato noodles combined with a mix of sautéed veggies and usually beef, and tossed in a sauce made from soy sauce, sesame oil, and just a touch of sugar. Sweet potato noodles remind me a bit of kelp noodles, which are made from kelp seaweed. I love kelp noodles because they function like pasta, but have almost zero calories (an entire 12-ounce bag has 18 calories), and they take on the flavor of whatever you mix them with.

I've cooked with kelp noodles many times, and after a few missteps, I've figured out how to make them perfectly. Straight out of the bag the noodles feel brittle, but the pro move is to toss them raw with your sauce of choice, and let the sauced noodles sit for about 3 hours; they will soften and become chewy. I've found that sauces with acid, like tomato sauce, work especially well. Here I've combined kelp noodles with the elements of japchae (minus the meat)—two of my favorite foods in one dish. As I mentioned, make these a few hours before you're planning to serve and let them marinate.

SERVES 4 TO 6

1 package (12 ounces) kelp noodles

3 teaspoons toasted sesame oil

2 tablespoons plus 1 teaspoon apple cider vinegar

2 tablespoons gluten-free soy sauce

1 teaspoon coconut palm sugar

¼ teaspoon freshly ground black pepper

2 tablespoons vegetable oil

2 cups thinly sliced green cabbage leaves

1 cup raw carrot matchsticks (from about ½ scrubbed, unpeeled carrot)

7 fresh shiitake mushrooms, cleaned, trimmed, and thinly sliced

4 scallions, roots trimmed, white and light green parts cut into 2-inch lengths

½ teaspoon minced garlic

1 cup packed fresh baby spinach leaves

2 teaspoons toasted sesame seeds (see page 161)

Olive oil for reheating (optional)

1. Place the kelp noodles in a large bowl. Rinse the noodles several times with tap water and drain well. Using kitchen scissors, roughly cut the noodles into 4-inch lengths. Add the sesame oil and toss to coat. Set aside.

2. Combine the apple cider vinegar, soy sauce, coconut palm sugar, and pepper in a small bowl and stir together with a fork. Set aside.

3. Heat a large pan over medium heat and add the vegetable oil. When the oil is hot, add the cabbage and carrot and sauté, stirring frequently, until the vegetables are shiny and slightly wilted, about 4 minutes. Add the mushrooms, scallions, and garlic and sauté, stirring frequently, until the scallions begin to wilt, about 4 more minutes. Turn off the heat and add the spinach and half of the reserved sauce and stir to combine. The spinach should wilt slightly

4. Pour the vegetable mixture over the kelp noodles in the bowl, add the remaining sauce, and toss to coat. Add the sesame seeds and toss again. Let the noodles sit for 3 hours to soften.

5. Serve at room temperature or reheat in a large pan with a splash of olive oil over medium heat until just warm.

Kelp Noodle Japchae will keep, in an airtight container in the refrigerator, for up to 2 days.

DRUNKEN CHICKPEA SPAGHETTI

Years ago I visited a restaurant in New York City named Felidia. There, for the first and only time in my life, I noticed a pasta dish on the menu that called for bucatini cooked in red wine, and out of pure curiosity I ordered it. It was incredible—the acidity in the pasta balanced by a rich sauce of melted butter, cheese, and black pepper. Inspired by that dining experience long ago, I've reworked that recipe into the following, which is dairy- and gluten-free.

I like to use Banza brand chickpea spaghetti (which is sold at natural foods supermarkets like Whole Foods) because it most closely approximates a classic pasta texture, but you could try other alt-pastas like those made from quinoa.

---

1. Bring a large pot of tap water to a boil over high heat. Salt it generously, add the pasta, and cook, stirring occasionally so it doesn't stick, until barely pliable and still hard in the center, about 1 minute. Drain in a colander.

2. Meanwhile, heat a large pan over medium-low heat and add ¼ cup of the olive oil, the garlic, and red pepper flakes. When the garlic begins to brown, sprinkle it with a pinch each of salt and black pepper, add the red wine, and bring to a boil. Add the parboiled pasta and cook, stirring occasionally, until the pasta is al dente and has absorbed the red wine, about 4 minutes. Remove the pan from the heat.

3. Add the remaining 1 tablespoon of olive oil, the parsley, pine nuts, lemon juice and zest, and stir to combine. Taste and add more lemon juice as needed. Serve immediately.

SERVES 3

Fine sea salt

½ pound chickpea spaghetti (see headnote)

¼ cup plus 1 tablespoon extra-virgin olive oil

½ tablespoon minced garlic

¼ teaspoon crushed red pepper flakes

Freshly ground black pepper

2 cups dry red wine (preferably vegan), such as Malbec

¼ cup finely chopped fresh flat-leaf (Italian) parsley leaves

¼ cup pine nuts, toasted (see page 161)

5 teaspoons fresh lemon juice, plus extra as needed

Freshly grated zest of 1 lemon

BEET FALAFEL WITH ROSE-PICKLED VEGGIES

Rather than simply serving a falafel made from chickpeas, I've added beets to make a fun red version of the Middle Eastern staple. Serve them on a plate beside the rose-pickled veggies—in a colorful combo of carrots, purple cabbage, and cucumber—or throw them all over cauliflower rice for a composed bowl. I really love the soft aromatic flavor of the pickle brine, which also lends itself well to other ingredients such as beans or onions. Once you've consumed all the pickles, feel free to experiment with the brine and add in other types of vegetables. (Note that you'll need to make the pickles about an hour in advance.)

MAKES ABOUT 16 PATTIES; SERVES 8

Coconut oil, for greasing the pan
⅓ cup fresh cilantro leaves
⅓ cup fresh flat-leaf (Italian) parsley leaves
⅓ cup fresh lemon juice
2 tablespoons seltzer water
2 cups cooked chickpeas
1 tablespoon ground psyllium husks
1 teaspoon freshly grated lemon zest
1 garlic clove, peeled
¾ cup chopped, peeled, cooked red beet (see page 68)
¼ teaspoon ground cumin
⅛ teaspoon ground coriander
⅛ teaspoon cayenne pepper
⅛ teaspoon baking soda
1½ teaspoons fine sea salt, or more to taste
⅛ teaspoon freshly ground black pepper
Rose-Pickled Veggies (recipe follows), for serving

1. Preheat the oven to 450°F. Grease a rimmed baking sheet with coconut oil.

2. Combine the cilantro, parsley, lemon juice, seltzer water, chickpeas, psyllium husks, lemon zest, garlic, beet, cumin, coriander, cayenne, baking soda, salt, and pepper in a food processor and process until smooth, scraping down the side as needed, about 90 seconds. Transfer the falafel mixture to a bowl, cover it, and refrigerate to bind the dough, about 20 minutes.

3. Remove the dough from the fridge. Scoop about 2 tablespoons of the dough into your hands and form it into a patty about ½ inch thick. Place it on the prepared baking sheet and repeat with the remaining dough.

4. Bake the patties for 15 minutes, then flip them

with a spatula and continue baking until they look dry, about 15 minutes more.

5. Serve immediately, with the rose-pickled veggies.

Beet Falafel will keep, in an airtight container in the refrigerator, for 2 days. Before serving, reheat the patties in a 350°F oven for 10 minutes.

ROSE-PICKLED VEGGIES

Combine the vinegars, filtered water, honey, rose petals, coriander seeds, pink peppercorns, caraway seeds, and salt in a medium bowl and stir until the honey is incorporated. Add the carrot, cabbage, and cucumber and stir to distribute. Let the vegetables pickle at room temperature for at least 1 hour and up to 2 hours (if pickling longer, cover the mixture and refrigerate it to prevent the pickle flavor from intensifying too quickly).

Rose-Pickled Veggies will keep, in their liquid in an airtight container in the refrigerator, for 1 year (really!).

MAKES ABOUT 1 CUP

½ cup white distilled vinegar

⅓ cup apple cider vinegar

¼ cup plus 1 tablespoon filtered water

2½ teaspoons raw honey

1 teaspoon dried rose petals (see page 32)

½ teaspoon whole coriander seeds

½ teaspoon pink peppercorns

½ teaspoon caraway seeds

½ teaspoon fine sea salt

¼ cup raw carrot matchsticks

¼ cup slivered red cabbage

¼ cup cucumber matchsticks

PINEAPPLE KIMCHI SUMMER SUNSET ROLLS

With their ombre pink hue, these beet-stained rolls remind me of a summer sunset. Of course if you don't want to take the extra step and tint the roll wrappers, that's entirely fine, but the tie-dye effect adds a fun, playful twist. Beyond their eye-catching presentation, these refreshing rolls pack punchy flavor thanks to the pineapple kimchi within. It's sweet, spicy, and sour all at the same time, with tons of taste from the gochugaru—a bright red powder made from Korean chile flakes. This recipe will make more pineapple kimchi than you need for the rolls; I like to add the leftovers to pretty much anything: atop veggie tacos, in a breakfast bowl, in place of salad dressing.

MAKES 18 ROLLS

For the Wrappers
1 medium raw red beet, unpeeled, scrubbed and cut into 6 pieces
18 spring roll rice wrappers (6 inches each; see Notes)
Black sesame seeds, for garnish

For the Pineapple Kimchi
1 medium pineapple
5 garlic cloves, peeled
1 small shallot, peeled
2-inch piece (about 1 ounce) fresh ginger, peeled and roughly chopped
3 tablespoons rice wine vinegar
1½ tablespoons gochugaru (see Notes)
½ teaspoon fine sea salt

For the Filling
2 cups mushrooms, such as shimeji, enoki, or shiitake, cleaned, bottoms trimmed
4½ teaspoons olive oil
Fine sea salt and freshly ground black pepper
2 tablespoons gluten-free soy sauce
2 medium carrots, peeled, trimmed, and cut into matchstick-size pieces
2 cups pea shoots
2 cups daikon, peeled and cut into matchstick-size pieces
1 bunch fresh cilantro, washed, 2 inches removed from stalks

1. Preheat the oven to 350°F.

2. Make the dye for the wrappers: Place the beet in a medium bowl and add 1⅓ cups hot tap water to cover. Set aside to steep while you assemble the remaining ingredients.

3. Make the pineapple kimchi: Cut off the crown and stem of the pineapple and discard. Positioning one cut side of the pineapple on a cutting board, and using a chef's knife, slice off the skin from top to bottom, cutting deeply enough to remove any eyes. Cut the pineapple vertically in half lengthwise and set aside one half. Cut one pineapple half into rough 1-inch cubes, making sure to cut around the tougher core. Transfer about 2½ cups of the pineapple cubes to a blender (if you have extra cubes, reserve them for another use). Quarter the remaining pineapple half lengthwise, slicing off and discarding the tough central core of each quarter. Slice each quarter into long strips about ⅛ inch thick and 4 inches long. Transfer these pieces to a large bowl and set aside.

4. Add the garlic, shallot, ginger, rice wine vinegar, gochugaru, and salt to the blender and blend until smooth, about 1 minute. Pour the pineapple kimchi over the pineapple strips and toss to coat. Set aside.

5. Make the filling: Toss the mushrooms with the olive oil in a medium bowl (if using shiitakes, slice them into quarters first). Spread the mushrooms in a single layer on a rimmed baking sheet and season generously with salt and pepper. Roast the mushrooms until soft, about 10 minutes. Remove the mushrooms from the oven and transfer them to a small bowl. Add the soy sauce and toss to coat. Set aside.

6. Dye the wrappers: Lay a clean, damp kitchen towel on a work surface. Place a medium, shallow bowl of warm water next to the work surface and the reserved beet water beside that (the beet water should still be warm; if it is not,

reheat it gently in a small pot or the microwave). Dip the right side of a wrapper in the warm water to cover it, then quickly dip the left side in the beet water; transfer the dipped wrapper to the damp towel. The wrapper should be just slightly pliable and tinted soft magenta on one side (it will be white on the other and will shade from white to pink as the wrapper continues to hydrate and the dye bleeds).

7. Assemble the summer rolls: Arrange a generous pinch each of the carrot, pea shoots, daikon, and cilantro about 1 inch from the bottom of the wrapper and across both the pink and white sides, leaving a border of about $1\frac{1}{2}$ inches on the pink side (this side will be wrapped up to form the base of the roll; the white side will be left open, allowing the veg to peek out). Top each mound of vegetables with about 1 tablespoon of mushrooms and 2 teaspoons of pineapple kimchi—be careful not to overfill it!

8. Fold the bottom of the wrapper up and over the filling to cover about

$\frac{1}{2}$ inch, then tuck the pink side of the wrapper over to close that end. Continue to roll tightly from the bottom up until the summer roll is wrapped and the vegetables peek out of the white side. Set the summer roll, seam side down, on a plate. Repeat with the remaining wrappers and filling.

9. Sprinkle the summer rolls with sesame seeds and serve immediately.

Pineapple Kimchi Summer Sunset Rolls will keep, in an airtight container in the refrigerator, for up to 2 days. The Pineapple Kimchi will keep, in an airtight container in the refrigerator, for up to 5 days.

Notes: Spring roll rice wrappers, which are sometimes labeled as "spring roll skin," can be purchased from Asian markets, many supermarkets, and online at Amazon.com, as can gochugaru. But note that some wrappers are made from rice while others are made from wheat. Make sure to read the product's ingredients to ensure you have the correct rice wrappers.

AVOCADO PIZZA WITH TOMATILLO SALSA

This recipe is inspired by an avocado pizza I tried at a restaurant in Mexico City called Huset. While Huset serves its avocado pizza on regular Neapolitan-style pizza dough, I've changed up the recipe to make a quick and easy crust that's gluten-free. I've also added tomatillo salsa for acidity. If you don't want to do the extra work and make tomatillo salsa, you can use store-bought or simply leave that out of the recipe and either add raw or roasted tomatoes, or just amp up the fresh lime juice. I like to eat this for a late lunch or cut it into eight slices as an appetizer. It's great both warm and at room temperature.

Note that because the crust is bound with psyllium (see page 11), it takes on a sort of chewy quality. The top will crisp up in the oven, but expect the bottom to stay soft.

MAKES TWO 8-INCH PIZZAS

For the Dough
1 tablespoon olive oil, plus extra for greasing the pan
½ cup pureed butternut squash or sweet potato, fresh or canned
¼ cup psyllium husks
¼ cup almond flour
¼ cup oat flour, plus extra as needed
2 tablespoons flax meal
1 teaspoon fine sea salt
¼ teaspoon freshly ground black pepper

For the Topping
2 avocados
2 teaspoons olive oil
2 tablespoons Tomatillo Salsa (page 164), plus extra as needed
1 to 2 jalapeños thinly sliced crosswise or minced and seeded
Fresh cilantro leaves or blossoms, for garnish
1 lime, halved
Coarse sea salt, for garnish

1. Make the dough: Preheat the oven to 375°F. Coat two rimmed baking sheets with olive oil.

2. Combine the squash, psyllium husks, almond flour, ¼ cup of the oat flour, the flax meal, the 1 tablespoon of olive oil, salt, and pepper in a medium bowl and, using a wooden spoon, mix until the ingredients are fully incorporated and form a slightly sticky, gel-like dough. Using your hands, divide the dough into two halves.

3. Sprinkle oat flour on a work surface and place one piece of the dough on top. Knead the dough a few

times, then shape it into a flat disk. Using a rolling pin dusted with oat flour, roll the dough into a rough circle about 8 inches wide and ¼ inch thick. Repeat with the remaining piece of dough. Carefully transfer the dough rounds to the prepared baking sheet and bake until lightly browned on top, about 10 minutes. Using a spatula, flip the crusts over, then bake until lightly brown on the second side (the tops will still feel slightly soft), 10 minutes more.

4. While the crusts bake, prepare the topping: Slice each avocado in half, lengthwise. Remove the pit.

Using your hands, carefully peel the skin away from the flesh and discard the skin. Place the avocado halves, cut side down, on a cutting board and slice them lengthwise into ⅛-inch-thick slices.

5. Remove the crusts from the oven and rub the top of each with 1 teaspoon of olive oil. Layer the avocado slices on top, then dot each with 1 tablespoon tomatillo salsa, and sprinkle 1 tablespoon minced jalapeño on each. Add a few cilantro leaves to each pizza as a garnish, squeeze the juice of half a lime atop each, and finish with a sprinkle of salt. Serve immediately.

BROCCOLI-AVOCADO SOUP

I usually make this soup in the summer because it's filling but light at the same time. And it's great both hot and at room temperature. I love crumbling a few tortilla chips on top, or even sprinkling on some corn nuts, but this soup is thick enough that you could serve it at a party as a healthy dip with tortilla chips.

SERVES 3

2 small heads broccoli

¼ cup fresh lime juice, plus extra as needed

1 avocado, halved, peeled, and pitted, plus extra sliced or chopped for garnish

1 garlic clove, peeled

¼ cup packed fresh cilantro leaves, plus 3 cilantro sprigs for garnish

1 tablespoon extra-virgin olive oil

½ teaspoon fine sea salt, plus extra as needed

Freshly ground black pepper

¼ cup crushed tortilla chips or corn nuts, for garnish

1. Fill a large pot with tap water to a depth of 2 inches and place it over medium-high heat. Remove and discard the bottom ½ inch of each broccoli stalk, and cut each head into 4 to 6 pieces. When the water comes to a simmer, add the broccoli, cover, and steam until bright green, about 4 minutes.

2. Using tongs or a fork, transfer the broccoli to a high-powered blender or food processor along with 1 cup of the cooking liquid (reserve the rest). Add the lime juice, avocado halves, garlic, cilantro leaves, olive oil, ½ teaspoon of salt, and pepper to taste, and blend until pureed, about 30 seconds. The soup should be thick and easily coat

the back of a spoon. If it's too thick, add the reserved broccoli cooking liquid, 1 tablespoon at a time until the desired thickness is reached. Taste and adjust the salt, pepper, and lime juice as needed.

3. Divide the soup among three bowls and garnish each with avocado slices, crushed tortilla chips, and a sprig of fresh cilantro.

Broccoli-Avocado Soup will keep, in an airtight container in the refrigerator, for up to 2 days. Reheat the leftovers before serving.

Let's

Get

Wasted

As much as I try to avoid kitchen waste, it's sometimes difficult to find new ways to use typically discarded ingredients. But I do try. For example, instead of tossing beet greens, I wash them and steam or sauté them like kale, and serve them with a splash of olive oil and vinegar or lemon juice. When I am cooking broccoli, I slice off the vegetable's long stalk, cut off its tough outer skin, and slice the stalk into coins, and I eat those with a squeeze of lemon and a pinch of salt—it's a snack my mother has served to me my whole life. If you're creative, there are many ways to give products you usually throw away new life. For example, kale stems—those tough stalks that are difficult to chew. This chapter offers recipes for a few ingredients you'd probably not think to consume—from those challenging kale stems to almond pulp left over from making homemade milks.

Sautéed Kale with Kale Stem–Cilantro Chimichurri

Salt and Pepper Almond Pulp Cracker Bread

Salty Cacao Almond Pulp Cracker Bread

Almond-Macadamia Crumble

Berry Pollen Power Bites

SAUTÉED KALE WITH KALE STEM-CILANTRO CHIMICHURRI

Over the summer, when I buy kale from New York's Union Square Greenmarket, once I stem the leaves, I snack on the leftover stems, sometimes with a squeeze of lemon and a pinch of salt. Sure, kale stems are tough, but they soften up if you cook them, so there's really no reason to discard them. Here, after separating the stems from the leaves I've boiled the stems and added them to a traditional Argentine sauce called chimichurri. Think olive oil, parsley, a touch of heat, and a tang from red wine vinegar. Most recipes call for oregano, but I've subbed in fresh cilantro instead. If you have any extra chimichurri after dressing the leaves, I recommend using it on roasted veggies or mixing it into a salad.

SERVES 6

For the Chimichurri
¼ teaspoon fine sea salt, plus extra for salting the water
Stems from 1 bunch lacinato kale, dry ends trimmed, sliced into 1-inch lengths (reserve the leaves for the sautéed kale)
1 garlic clove, peeled
¼ cup packed fresh flat-leaf (Italian) parsley leaves
⅛ cup packed fresh cilantro leaves
1 tablespoon red wine vinegar
1 teaspoon fresh lime juice
¼ teaspoon crushed red pepper flakes
⅛ teaspoon freshly ground black pepper
¼ cup plus 2 tablespoons olive oil

For the Sautéed Kale
1 tablespoon olive oil, plus extra for garnish
1 garlic clove, thinly sliced
⅛ teaspoon crushed red pepper flakes
Pinch of fine sea salt
6 packed cups trimmed kale leaves
Freshly ground black pepper, for garnish (optional)

1. Make the chimichurri: Place a medium pot of tap water with a pinch of salt over medium-high heat and bring to a boil. Add the kale stems and cook until softened, about 10 minutes. Strain the kale stems in a colander and transfer them to a food processor.

2. Add the garlic and process until the stems are broken down, about 2 minutes. Add the parsley, cilantro, red wine vinegar, lime juice, red pepper flakes, black pepper, ¼ teaspoon of salt, and 3 tablespoons of olive oil and process until fully incorporated, about 1 minute. Transfer the mixture to a medium bowl and stir in the remaining 3 tablespoons of olive oil. Set aside. (Chimichurri will keep, in an airtight container in the refrigerator, for about 2 days.)

3. Make the sautéed kale: Heat 1 tablespoon of olive oil in a large pan over medium heat and add the garlic, red pepper flakes, and salt. Stir until the garlic becomes fragrant, about 1 minute; do not brown the garlic. Add the kale and about ¾ cup tap water and steam, covered, adding more water as necessary to cook the kale, until it's soft and the water has evaporated, about 10 minutes. Remove the kale from the heat and stir in the chimichurri to taste.

4. Transfer the dressed kale to a platter, top with a drizzle of olive oil, and sprinkle with freshly ground black pepper if desired. Serve immediately.

SALT AND PEPPER ALMOND PULP CRACKER BREAD

I am always looking for new ways to repurpose the surplus almond pulp left over from making milk. And this recipe yields a superthin flatbread-like cracker that's a bit crisp, but still pliable, almost like a wrap. I like to tear it roughly with my hands and top it with avocado, a pinch of salt, and the Pastrami Spice blend on page 173. Here, you'll see two versions of the recipe, one with more savory ingredients, the other with cacao and a bit of honey.

MAKES ONE 9 × 8-INCH SHEET

½ cup wet almond pulp (left over from making 1 almond milk recipe, see page 28)
4½ teaspoons olive oil
1½ teaspoons ground flax meal
½ teaspoon fine sea salt
¼ teaspoon filtered water
Pinch of freshly ground black pepper

1. Preheat the oven to 350°F. Lay a sheet of parchment paper on a work surface.

2. Combine all the ingredients in a medium bowl and stir until fully incorporated. The dough should feel soft and moist; if it feels dry, add water, ⅛ teaspoon at a time, until it's hydrated and can form a ball.

3. Transfer the dough to the parchment paper and place a second sheet of parchment paper atop. Using a rolling pin, roll the dough between the parchment to a thickness of ⅛ to 1/16 inch. Peel off the top layer of parchment and transfer the parchment with the dough onto a baking sheet and into the oven.

4. Bake until the dough is light brown around the edges, about 9 minutes. Using a spatula, carefully flip the dough. Return it to the oven and bake until it is golden brown, about 4 minutes more. Let cool on the parchment paper.

Salt and Pepper Almond Pulp Cracker Bread will keep, covered at room temperature, for about 2 days.

Variation

Salty Cacao Almond Pulp Cracker Bread: This cracker isn't sweet; in fact, it's just about as savory as the original recipe. Feel free to top it with avocado, or go for a sweeter twist with almond butter and banana or fresh raspberries and tahini. Substitute melted coconut oil for the olive oil, omit the pepper, and add 1½ teaspoons raw cacao powder and ½ teaspoon raw honey to the dough.

ALMOND-MACADAMIA CRUMBLE

There are so many ways to use this versatile crumble. I've eaten it for breakfast as a fresh granola-like cereal mixed with some oats, and I've shaped it into balls and frozen them as a quick snack. You can press the crumble into the bottom of a tart mold and use it as the base for a dessert, or eat it straight out of the jar! Or atop ice cream (see page 144). It's addictive!

Combine all the ingredients in a food processor and blend until the macadamia nuts are broken down into a coarse meal, about 30 seconds.

Almond-Macadamia Crumble will keep, in an airtight container in the freezer, for about 3 months. Bring to room temperature before using.

MAKES 2⅔ CUPS

1 cup macadamia nuts
¾ cup moist almond pulp
   (left over from making
   1 almond milk recipe,
   see page 28)
½ cup coconut butter
¼ cup coconut palm sugar
3 tablespoons mesquite powder
2 tablespoons hemp seeds
1 tablespoon flax meal
1 tablespoon ground cinnamon
1 tablespoon cacao nibs
2 teaspoons pure vanilla extract
¼ teaspoon fine sea salt

Make It Magical
Add 1 tablespoon tocos and/or 1 teaspoon reishi or cordyceps before blending.

Almonds are more fibrous than other nuts, which is why there's always a ton of pulp left over when preparing almond milk. Since almonds are so pricey these days, I've played around with different ways to reuse the leftover meal. Sometimes I add it to baked goods like morning muffins, and I've even turned the meal into a streusel to top chia pudding. But this is one of my favorite super-simple ways to repurpose pulp into a tasty, energy-boosting snack that's a touch chewy and filled with fiber.

MAKES 36 BITES

1 cup plus 3 tablespoons leftover almond meal or almond flour (see Notes)

¼ cup plus 2 tablespoons coconut oil, melted

3 tablespoons shredded unsweetened coconut

3 tablespoons cacao nibs

3 tablespoons dried goji berries

3 tablespoons raw honey

1 tablespoon hemp seeds

¼ teaspoon fine sea salt

1 tablespoon black sesame seeds

1 tablespoon flax meal

1 tablespoon coconut butter

½ cup freeze-dried raspberries, crushed into a semifine dust (some chunks will remain)

⅓ cup bee pollen

1. Combine the almond meal, coconut oil, shredded coconut, cacao nibs, goji berries, honey, hemp seeds, salt, black sesame seeds, flax meal, and coconut butter in a medium bowl and stir to blend. Transfer the bowl to the fridge and chill until the dough is cold and firm like traditional cookie dough, about 30 minutes.

2. Meanwhile, place the crushed, freeze-dried raspberries in a small bowl, and the bee pollen in another.

3. Remove the chilled dough from the refrigerator and, using a teaspoon, scoop a ball of the dough into your hands. Roll the dough between your hands to form a compact ball. Place the dough ball in the raspberry powder and toss to coat well. Next, dip one side of the dough ball into the bee pollen to coat half of it, then use your hands to press the pollen into the ball and make sure it sticks. Place the energy bite on a plate and repeat with the remaining dough, raspberry dust, and bee pollen.

Berry Pollen Power Bites will keep, covered in the refrigerator, for up to 5 days.

Notes: When making almond milk, about 1 cup of almonds will yield about ½ cup of leftover pulp. If you don't have any pulp on hand, you can buy almond meal at grocery stores or online.

Four

SNACKS+ SWEETS

Broccomole

Beet Hummus

Roasted Purple Yam with Coconut, Lime, and Tahini

Roasted Sweet Potatoes with Black Honey Tahini, Dukkah, and Dill

Seeded Nori Crisps

Medicine Bread

Miso-Almond Cookies with Date Caramel Glaze

Matcha Cookies with Cardamom, Orange, and Toasted Pistachios

Chamomile Milk Tea Pudding with Fennel and Pistachios

Fudgy Pronuts with Spiced Coffee-Cacao Glaze

Vanilla Berry Morning Cakes

Lisa Frank Mountain Cake

Raw-Cacao-Banana "Ice Cream" with Almond-Macadamia Crumble

Kiwi–Passion Fruit Vegan Cheesecake Bars

Strawberry–Pink Peppercorn "Ice Cream" Sticks

Wasabi Fudge Pops

Dirty Chai Tahini Cups

Whether you're in the mood for seaweed crackers or energy-boosting frozen chai-spiced coconut cups, this chapter is where you'll find both sweet and savory "snacky" things.

There's a nutty Medicine Bread (page 125) that you could transform into a sandwich, or eat with a smear of Matcha Honey Butter (page 161) or Strawberry-Vanilla Bean Chia Jam (page 158) in the morning or afternoon. Many of the recipes herein, such as the Roasted Purple Yam with Coconut, Lime, and Tahini (page 121), are versatile in the sense that you can eat them at different points of the day—that's even true for the "desserts," which incorporate small amounts of natural sweeteners.

About those sweet treats: As I mentioned in the introduction, I've omitted white sugar from this book because it's an empty source of sweetness with zero nutritional value—I figure if you're going to have sugar, at least take it from natural sources, and in the most minimally refined form possible. While sugar is sugar regardless of the source, if you're eating fruit sugar, or an unprocessed sweetener like raw honey, you're at least getting additional vitamins, minerals, and other health benefits with your dose of sweet. The dessert-like snacks within this chapter, from Strawberry-Pink Peppercorn "Ice Cream" Sticks (page 148) to Matcha Cookies with Cardamom, Orange, and Toasted Pistachios (page 130), only call for fruit and other less manipulated sweeteners to create uniquely flavored, satiating foods. Each will curb a sugar craving—with added nutrients to boot!

BROCCOMOLE

When broccoli meets avocado . . . broccomole is born! I remember trying a great version of "healthier" guac cut with peas at a spa in Tijuana, Mexico, called Rancho La Puerta. Which made me think . . . what else could you mix into guacamole? Broccoli, a vegetable that I love, quickly came to mind. Here, you're still getting the classic guac flavors in a dip that's a bit lighter than what you'd typically expect. I've also added a red chile for heat, but if you prefer not to make this dish spicy, you can leave it out. Thai basil contributes an extra flavor dimension, but you can easily swap in Italian basil or omit it entirely.

Note that you'll want to eat this right after you make it as it doesn't keep well.

MAKES ABOUT 1⅓ CUPS

3 cups cooked broccoli florets (from about 2 small heads)

1 avocado, pitted, flesh scooped out

¼ cup fresh lime juice

3 tablespoons coarsely chopped, packed fresh cilantro leaves

1 scallion, trimmed

1 tablespoon coarsely chopped red onion

1 tablespoon filtered water

1 tablespoon coarsely chopped freah Thai basil leaves (optional)

1 teaspoon fine sea salt

¾ medium fresh red chile, stemmed and halved (seeds removed for less heat if desired; optional)

¼ teaspoon freshly ground black pepper

Combine the broccoli, avocado, lime juice, cilantro, scallion, red onion, filtered water, basil, salt, chile (if using), and black pepper in a food processor and puree until the ingredients are fully broken down and the broccomole is light and smooth, about 3 minutes. Serve immediately.

BEET HUMMUS

I'm sort of obsessed with this hummus. Right off the bat, I am going to tell you there's way more acid in this recipe than in traditional hummus; the extra lemon juice makes sense because it brightens the savory tahini, as does the salt. Serve this beside a beautiful crudité assortment fresh from the market.

....

Combine the chickpeas, beet, lemon juice, garlic, tahini, olive oil, filtered water, coriander, and salt in a food processor or blender and process until the mixture is smooth and bright pink, about 2 minutes. Season to taste with salt. Scrape the hummus into a bowl and sprinkle with black sesame seeds if desired.

Beet Hummus will keep, in an airtight container in the refrigerator, for 2 days.

MAKES ABOUT 1¾ CUPS

1 cup canned chickpeas
1 peeled, cooked red beet
    (about 4 ounces), coarsely
    chopped (to equal ½ cup)
¼ cup fresh lemon juice
1 garlic clove, peeled
½ cup tahini (sesame paste)
¼ cup extra-virgin olive oil
1 tablespoon filtered water
3 teaspoons ground coriander
¾ teaspoon fine sea salt, plus
    extra as needed
Black sesame seeds, for garnish
    (optional)

ROASTED PURPLE YAM WITH COCONUT, LIME, AND TAHINI

I love the slightly tropical flavor of this simple dish. You've got the natural sweet caramel flavor from the yam, mixed with coconut for an extra exotic note and acidity to brighten. Tahini mellows the potato's sweetness with an additional creamy note.

SERVES 2 TO 4

2 medium purple yams

2 tablespoons coconut oil

2 teaspoons tahini (sesame paste)

½ lime, plus extra for serving

1 teaspoon bee pollen

¼ teaspoon fine sea salt

1. Preheat the oven to 350°F. Line a rimmed baking sheet with parchment paper.

2. Prick the yams all over with a fork, place them on the baking sheet, and roast in the oven until soft when pierced in the middle with a fork, about 25 minutes. Set the yams aside to cool slightly.

3. Using a paring knife, carefully peel the yams while they're still hot; discard the skins. Slice the yams in half lengthwise and transfer them to a platter (or individual plates). Using a fork, gently press the yam halves into the plate(s), mashing them slightly.

4. Add 1½ teaspoons of the coconut oil to each yam half, distributing the oil evenly with a knife to coat the yam. Drizzle each yam half with ½ teaspoon of tahini, then squeeze the lime half evenly over each and grate the lime zest atop. Finally, top each with ¼ teaspoon of the bee pollen and a pinch of salt. Serve immediately with the remaining lime alongside.

ROASTED SWEET POTATOES WITH BLACK HONEY TAHINI, DUKKAH, AND DILL

Both sweet and savory, with a spark of freshness from the dill, this warming potato dish could be consumed for lunch or as an afternoon snack. The black honey tahini offers a rich, creamy texture, while the dukkah—an Egyptian spice blend—adds a hit of umami and spice thanks to its toasted medley of ingredients. While I call for homemade tahini and dukkah, you can purchase both in supermarkets and specialty stores. So if you don't want to make your own (which I'd still encourage you do), then you can simplify this recipe by subbing in store-bought.

SERVES 2 TO 4

2 medium sweet potatoes, scrubbed
2 teaspoons olive oil
1 to 2 tablespoons Black Honey Tahini (page 160)
1 tablespoon Dukkah (page 171)
4½ teaspoons chopped fresh dill
Fine sea salt and freshly ground black pepper

1. Preheat the oven to 400°F. Line a rimmed bakng sheet with parchment paper.

2. Prick the sweet potatoes all over with a fork, place them on the baking sheet, and roast in the oven until soft when pierced in the middle with a fork, about 1 hour.

3. Carefully transfer the sweet potatoes to a cutting board and use a paring knife to halve them lengthwise. Transfer them to a platter (or individual plates) and drizzle each half with ½ teaspoon of the olive oil and a quarter of the black honey tahini. Sprinkle the potatoes evenly with the dukkah, dill, and salt and pepper to taste. Serve hot.

SEEDED NORI CRISPS

Nori is the Japanese name for a type of dried seaweed that's pressed into sheets and is commonly used in sushi. It's also becoming increasingly popular as a healthy snack food, one that contains B vitamins, trace minerals, and unsaturated fatty acids—and a box of which you can hoover through in a matter of seconds. Thanks to a layer of seeds, these nori crisps are a bit more substantial. Try them as a daytime snack (they're great), or bring them on a flight as a healthier answer to typical airplane food. For a dinner party appetizer, serve them beside the Beet Hummus on page 118.

page 118.

**MAKES FOUR
8 × 7-INCH SHEETS**

Coconut oil, for greasing the baking sheet
1 cup filtered water
1 cup flaxseeds
3 tablespoons chia seeds
3 tablespoons raw, unsalted sunflower seeds
3 tablespoons pumpkin seeds
3 tablespoons sesame seeds
1½ teaspoons fine sea salt
4 sheets dried nori (see Note)

1. Preheat the oven to 250°F. Line a rimmed baking sheet with parchment paper and grease the paper lightly with coconut oil.

2. Combine the filtered water, flaxseeds, and chia seeds in a large bowl and stir together. Let stand, stirring every 5 minutes or so, to hydrate the seeds, about 20 minutes.

3. Add the sunflower seeds, pumpkin seeds, sesame seeds, and salt to the hydrated seeds and stir to blend.

4. Arrange the nori on the prepared baking sheet. Divide the seed mixture among the four sheets of nori, using a spoon to smooth it evenly so that there's about $\frac{1}{8}$ inch of the mixture completely covering the nori.

5. Bake until the seeds are crispy, about 45 minutes. Using a spatula, flip the nori carefully, and continue baking until it is almost completely dry and the edges curl upward, about 45 minutes more.

Seeded Nori Crisps will keep, in an airtight container at room temperature, for up to 1 week.

Note: Dried nori sheets can be found at Asian and health food markets.

MEDICINE BREAD

A fter returning from a trip to Copenhagen, where dense, seed-studded rye bread is a staple, I wanted to create a version that was absent flour and heavy on nuts and seeds. This bread is it—inspired by an amazing recipe from the blog *My New Roots*, which I tweaked to add extra umami. If you want a sweeter version, try adding eight diced, pitted dates or two extra-soft bananas to the dough.

This makes for an awesome breakfast, especially with a smear of Matcha Honey Butter (page 161).

MAKES ONE
10 × 7-INCH LOAF

3 tablespoons melted coconut oil, plus extra for greasing the pan
1½ cups old-fashioned rolled oats
¾ cup raw, unsalted sunflower seeds
½ cup flax meal
½ cup raw hazelnuts
¼ cup raw almonds
¼ cup raw whole macadamia nuts
¼ cup psyllium husks
3 tablespoons chia seeds
1½ teaspoons fine sea salt
1 tablespoon pure maple syrup
1½ cups filtered water
Matcha Honey Butter, for serving (optional but recommended!)

1. Preheat the oven to 375°F. Grease a loaf pan with coconut oil.

2. Place the oats, sunflower seeds, flax meal, hazelnuts, almonds, macadamia nuts, psyllium husks, chia seeds, and salt in a large bowl and stir to combine.

3. Place the maple syrup, coconut oil, and filtered water in a medium bowl and stir to combine.

4. Add the wet ingredients to the dry ingredients and stir to blend until a thick, dense dough forms. Scrape the dough into the prepared pan, lay a sheet of waxed paper on top, and press down on the paper to spread the dough into the pan. Remove the waxed

paper and let the dough rest on the counter for 20 minutes.

5. Bake until the bread is light brown on top, about 20 minutes. Remove the bread from the oven and let it cool. Run a paring knife around the edges to loosen it from the pan. Wearing oven mitts, place a baking sheet over the bread and carefully flip the bread over onto the baking sheet. Return the bread to the oven and bake until lightly brown, 35 minutes more.

6. Let the bread cool to the touch (it will still be warm) before slicing. Serve warm or at room temperature, slathered with matcha honey butter if you wish.

Medicine Bread will keep, covered in plastic wrap in the refrigerator, for up to 1 week, or wrapped in aluminum foil and frozen in a ziplock bag for up to 2 months. Toast the chilled or frozen bread before serving.

MISO-ALMOND COOKIES WITH DATE CARAMEL GLAZE

Miso paste is an amazing ingredient that adds umami to sweet and savory dishes. When I see a miso dessert on any menu—anywhere, anytime—I will absolutely order it. These cookies call for a sweet-style white miso, which adds a unique savory element. However, these rounds still taste like a dessert since they incorporate coconut palm sugar and almond extract, which complement the miso's subtle nutty quality. A final glaze made from maple syrup and dates further enhances the cookies' nuttiness and depth of flavor.

MAKES 16 COOKIES

½ cup melted coconut oil or vegetable oil, plus extra for greasing the baking sheet

½ cup coconut palm sugar

2 tablespoons white miso paste (see Note)

¼ teaspoon pure almond extract

1 Chia Egg (page 12)

¾ cup brown rice flour

¾ cup almond flour

½ teaspoon baking soda

7 pitted dates

⅓ cup pure maple syrup

⅓ cup filtered water

Sesame seeds, for garnish

1. Preheat the oven to 325°F. Grease a rimmed baking sheet with coconut oil.

2. Combine the coconut oil, coconut palm sugar, miso paste, and almond extract in the bowl of a stand mixer fitted with the paddle attachment (or in a large bowl if using a handheld electric mixer) and blend at high speed until a light brown batter forms. Add the chia egg and stir with a wooden spoon to combine. Stir in the flours and baking soda until a thick, light brown dough forms.

3. Using a tablespoon, scoop mounds of the dough onto the prepared baking sheet, spacing them evenly, about 1½ inches apart. Bake until the cookies are lightly browned, 12 to 14 minutes. Let cool on the baking sheet.

4. Meanwhile, make the date caramel: Combine the dates and maple syrup in a small saucepan over

medium-low heat and cook, stirring occasionally, until the dates are tender, about 4 minutes. Transfer the mixture to a high-powered blender or a food processor, add the filtered water, and process until a smooth glaze forms, about 30 seconds.

5. Place the cookies on a plate and brush half of each cookie with the date caramel, then sprinkle sesame seeds on top of the glaze.

Miso-Almond Cookies with Date Caramel Glaze will keep, in an airtight container at room temperature, for 3 days.

Note: White miso, also called *shiro miso* in Japanese, is made from fermented soy beans and rice. Its mild flavor and sweetness come from a shorter fermentation period than that for other types of miso, which can have strong, funky flavor profiles.

MATCHA COOKIES WITH CARDAMOM, ORANGE, AND TOASTED PISTACHIOS

I've been addicted to matcha ever since I discovered the sweet grassy tea at New York tea parlor Cha-An over a decade ago. Now, beyond drinking the tea, I add it to different types of sweet and savory foods. In this recipe, I take inspiration from Middle Eastern flavors like cardamom, orange, and pistachio, and marry them with the subtle vegetal flavor of matcha.

1. Preheat the oven to 375°F and line a rimmed baking sheet with parchment paper.

2. Whisk together the flours, matcha, salt, baking soda, cardamom, and cinnamon in a medium bowl and set aside.

3. Combine the coconut palm sugar, mashed avocado, oil, and vanilla in a large bowl, and beat with an electric mixer on high speed until creamy and smooth, about 2 minutes. Add the orange zest and dates and beat just to incorporate.

4. Beat the flour mixture into the sugar mixture in 2 additions. Stir in the pistachios. The dough will appear shiny, thick, and tacky, almost like marzipan.

5. Using a tablespoon, scoop a portion of the dough into your hand and roll it between your palms to form a compact ball. Press each ball against your other palm and flatten it into a ¼-inch-thick disk. Place the disks onto the prepared baking sheet, spacing them evenly apart. (The cookies won't spread during baking.)

MAKES 25 COOKIES

¾ cup sweet rice flour (see Notes)
¾ cup almond flour
½ cup chestnut flour (see Notes)
2½ teaspoons matcha powder
1 teaspoon kosher salt
¾ teaspoon baking soda
1¼ teaspoons ground cardamom
¼ teaspoon ground cinnamon
½ cup coconut palm sugar
⅓ cup mashed avocado (½ medium avocado or about 2 ounces)
⅓ cup vegetable or olive oil
1 teaspoon pure vanilla extract
1 tablespoon freshly grated orange zest, plus extra for garnish
¼ cup chopped pitted dates (about 4 dates)
½ cup shelled pistachios, toasted (see page 161) and chopped

6. Bake, rotating the pan halfway through the baking time, until the cookies show subtle cracks on top (they may brown just slightly), 8 to 10 minutes. Let cool on the baking sheet for about 5 minutes. I like to sprinkle or grate a bit of fresh orange zest atop before serving.

Pro tip: When these cookies first come out of the oven, they are soft and delicate. But leave them out overnight, loosely covered with plastic wrap, and they will firm up into a chewy texture. And after three days, they are awesome dipped in coffee or tea as an afternoon snack.

Matcha Cookies with Cardamom, Orange, and Toasted Pistachios will keep, in a covered or uncovered container at room temperature, for 5 days.

Notes: Sweet rice flour, commonly used in sweet and savory Japanese dishes, is made from glutinous rice aka "sticky rice." When used in large quantities, this flour adds a chewy texture (it's what mochi is made from) and can help thicken and bind ingredients.

Chestnut flour, sometimes used in Italian desserts, is a soft white flour made from roasted, ground chestnuts. You can buy it at some Italian markets and online at Amazon.com.

CHAMOMILE MILK TEA PUDDING WITH FENNEL AND PISTACHIOS

Here the subtle flavor of chamomile is infused into a simple pudding and enhanced by hazelnut and orange. While the fennel and pistachio garnish is totally optional, it does make for a pretty presentation. If you want your fennel to sport an ombré look, drop a bit of beet juice or dehydrated beet powder atop the slices before baking (see Variation).

SERVES 4

2 cups Hazelnut Milk (see page 33) or other nut milk

⅓ cup cornstarch

¾ cup coconut cream (see page 9)

3 tablespoons dry chamomile tea

2 medium oranges, zested and juiced

6 tablespoons raw honey

¼ teaspoon fine sea salt

⅛ teaspoon freshly ground black pepper

¼ fennel bulb, fronds removed, bulb trimmed (optional)

2 tablespoons chopped toasted pistachios (see page 161), for garnish (optional)

1. Combine 1 cup of the hazelnut milk and the cornstarch in a medium bowl and whisk to incorporate. Set aside.

2. Place the remaining 1 cup of hazelnut milk, the coconut cream, and chamomile in a medium saucepan over medium heat and cook, stirring often (the mixture should not come to a boil), until it is thick and coats the back of a spoon, about 10 minutes.

3. Position a fine-mesh strainer over a heat-resistant bowl and pour the heated milk mixture through it, straining out and discarding the tea. Return the milk mixture to the saucepan. Add half of the orange zest, half of the orange juice, 4 tablespoons of the honey, salt, and pepper and cook, stirring constantly, over medium-high heat until the mixture thickens enough to coat the back of a spoon, about 5 minutes. Pour the pudding into a large bowl, cover it with plastic wrap touching the surface to prevent a skin from forming, and refrigerate until chilled, at least 2 hours (or up to 1 day if you wish to make it ahead).

4. Meanwhile, to make the fennel garnish (if using),

preheat the oven to 350°F. Line a rimmed baking sheet with parchment paper. Using a mandoline, thinly shave the fennel lengthwise into 4 pieces about $\frac{1}{8}$ inch thick. (Reserve the rest of the fennel for another use.) Combine the remaining orange juice and zest and 2 tablespoons of honey in a small bowl and stir to mix. Dip the fennel slices into the juice mixture to coat on both sides, then place them on the prepared baking sheet. Bake until the fennel looks slightly shriveled and dry, about 10 minutes. Let cool on the baking sheet.

5. To serve, spoon the pudding into four individual bowls. Sprinkle each with pistachios (if desired) and decorate with 1 slice of the fennel.

Chamomile Milk Tea pudding will keep, ungarnished, in an airtight container in the refrigerator, for 1 day.

Variation

Tie-Dyed Fennel: It's simple to tint the fennel pink, and that can be achieved one of two ways. You can make a magenta beet dye (see page 21) and, using a pastry brush, coat the tips of the fennel slices with the dye before baking. Or, again before baking, simply sprinkle $\frac{1}{8}$ teaspoon of dehydrated beet powder atop the tips of each fennel slice and massage it in with your fingers. Regardless of which method you use, the magenta color will fade slightly in the oven, but still maintain a pretty soft pink hue.

FUDGY PRONUTS WITH SPICED COFFEE-CACAO GLAZE

*P*ronut is a portmanteau of "protein" and "donut," and in addition to incorporating actual protein powder, it also packs protein-rich ingredients such as chia seeds and almonds. I like the chocolate-almond flavor that these rich, fudgy pronuts offer, which is enhanced with a chocolatey, subtly cinnamon-y donut glaze and toasted, chopped almonds. For a pop of color, try tossing the almonds in matcha powder, or topping the pronuts with colorful blossoms—or both. I use a silicone donut mold with wells that are about 2¾ inches in diameter.

1. Make the pronuts: Preheat the oven to 350°F.

2. Stir together the coconut palm sugar, coconut oil, chia eggs, almond butter, vanilla, baking powder, salt, and cacao powder in a large bowl to combine. Stir in the protein powder, oat flour, and coconut flour; the mixture will be thick and shiny. Using a spoon, divide the dough among the wells of the donut mold.

3. Bake the pronuts until they are light brown and cooked through (you'll need to cut into one with the tip of a knife to test), about 15 minutes. Let cool in the molds, then transfer to a plate or cutting board to decorate.

4. Make the glaze: Melt the chocolate in a double boiler over low heat. Whisk in the coffee, almond butter, coconut butter, vanilla, maple syrup, cinnamon, and salt until a smooth glaze forms. Remove from the heat.

MAKES 12 SMALL PRONUTS

For the Pronuts
¾ cup coconut palm sugar
½ cup coconut oil, melted
2 Chia Eggs (page 12)
6 tablespoons almond butter
2 teaspoons pure vanilla extract
¾ teaspoon baking powder
½ teaspoon fine sea salt
½ cup raw cacao powder
¼ cup protein powder
¼ cup oat flour
¼ cup coconut flour

For the Glaze and Garnish
3 ounces raw chocolate
6 tablespoons strong brewed coffee, at room temperature
3 teaspoons almond butter
2 tablespoons coconut butter
2 teaspoons pure vanilla extract
2 teaspoons pure maple syrup
¼ teaspoon ground cinnamon
Pinch of fine sea salt
1 tablespoon chopped toasted almonds (see page 161; toss with ¼ teaspoon matcha powder, if desired), for garnish
Edible flowers, for garnish (optional)

5. Using a large spoon, spoon the glaze evenly over the pronuts to cover the tops. Sprinkle on the nuts or edible flowers before the glaze sets. Serve immediately.

Fudgy Pronuts with Spiced Coffee-Cacao Glaze will keep, wrapped in plastic and refrigerated, for 2 days; let the glaze set before wrapping them.

VANILLA BERRY MORNING CAKES

I've already mentioned that Axe was one of my favorite restaurants when I lived in Venice, California, though sadly it's now shuttered. During my time in Venice, I could be found having brunch there every Saturday or Sunday morning, and I loved the place so much I'd sometimes go for dinner, too. Axe used to serve a thick, fudgy brownie dessert presented in a bowl surrounded by a shallow pool of milk—the dairy's creaminess helping to balance out the chocolate's richness. I love the idea of serving sweets in a pool of milk, and that inspired my use of almond milk here. While these Morning Cakes are not fudgy (since there's no chocolate involved), they're rich in a different way. Both the berries and chopped almonds add moisture and a buttery quality to the vanilla bean–flavored cake. You can serve this dish as dessert, but it's also amazing for breakfast. Since the cakes are delicate, they break apart easily, absorbing whatever is around them. Think of this as the freshest form of cereal and fruit you'll find.

MAKES 12 CAKES

⅔ cup solid coconut oil, plus extra for greasing the pan
¾ cup diced strawberries
½ cup raspberries
16 organic raw almonds, finely chopped
¾ cup plus 3 tablespoons coconut palm sugar
½ vanilla bean, seeds scraped out (pod reserved for another use)
2 Chia Eggs (page 12)
½ teaspoon fine sea salt
1¼ cups gluten-free all-purpose flour
1 teaspoon baking powder
Vanilla Bean–Almond Milk (page 28), for serving (optional)
Crumbled freeze-dried strawberries, for garnish (optional)

1. Preheat the oven to 375°F. Grease a muffin tin with coconut oil.

2. Prepare the fruit topping: Place the strawberries, raspberries, chopped almonds, 3 tablespoons of coconut palm sugar, and vanilla seeds in a medium bowl and stir to combine. Divide the fruit mixture evenly among the wells of the muffin tin.

3. Prepare the batter: Combine the remaining ¾ cup of coconut palm sugar and the coconut oil in the bowl of a stand

mixer fitted with the whisk attachment (or in a large bowl, if using a handheld electric mixer) and whisk until creamy, about 1 minute. Add the chia eggs and salt and whisk to incorporate. In a separate medium bowl, combine the gluten-free flour and baking powder and whisk together. Pour the flour mixture into the coconut palm sugar mixture and whisk to combine.

4. Divide the batter evenly among the wells of the muffin tin.

5. Bake until the cakes are light brown and cooked through (they will still be moist), about 28 minutes. Allow the cakes to cool a bit in the tin.

6. Using a large spoon, carefully scoop out the cakes from the pan (only remove as many as you plan to serve; they begin to lose their shape once removed from the pan). Place each cake, fruit side up, in the center of a small bowl (note that the cakes will be crumbly and delicate). Drizzle 4½ teaspoons of almond milk atop each. The almond milk will soak the cake and form a pool around it. Serve immediately garnished with freeze-dried strawberries, if desired.

Vanilla Berry Morning Cakes will keep (without the almond milk), wrapped individually in plastic wrap and stored in an airtight container, in the refrigerator for 3 days, or in the freezer for 1 month. Unwrap them and reheat them in the oven before serving.

LISA FRANK MOUNTAIN CAKE

This recipe was born from an experiment. I woke up one morning, wildly hungover, craving something cold and sweet. Scanning my kitchen, I noticed I had cashews and some almond milk lying around, in addition to a few bags of frozen fruit. I threw a bunch of ingredients together in an effort to create a layer cake, but before I actually created the layers, I decided to color them in various hues. I didn't expect this cake to be anything special, and when it came out of the freezer it looked like a mess. But after slicing it, I realized all the colors had created a pretty mountain effect, and both the look and palette reminded me of Lisa Frank, the vibrantly hued brand of rainbow and unicorn illustrations that colored my folders and notebooks in middle school. In addition to its eye-catching design, this cake is lusciously cool and creamy and comes with an added bonus: It's filled with wellness-promoting ingredients!

I should note that this cake will look slightly different every time you make it. That's because the peaks and valleys of the mountain layers depend on where you drop the different colors of cream. But I'd love to see how yours comes out, so tag me on The Gram: @kat_odell and @unicornfoods.

MAKES ONE 7 × 10-INCH CAKE; SERVES 20

For the Cake
Coconut oil, for greasing the baking dish
1 cup packed pitted dates
Filtered water (optional)
⅓ cup coconut butter
2 tablespoons fresh lemon juice
2 teaspoons pure vanilla extract
¼ teaspoon fine sea salt
1 cup frozen blueberries
2 cups almond flour

For the Cream
1 cup raw/organic cashews, soaked in water to cover for at least 4 hours or overnight, drained
1 cup coconut milk or nut milk of your choice
2 tablespoons raw honey
1 tablespoon fresh lemon juice
⅛ teaspoon fine sea salt
2 tablespoons coconut butter
2 tablespoons coconut flour
¼ teaspoon Blue Majik
½ teaspoon freeze-dried pitaya powder
1 teaspoon freeze-dried beet powder
1½ teaspoons bee pollen, plus extra for garnish

1. Grease a 10 × 7-inch baking dish with coconut oil.

2. Make the cake: Place the dates in a food processor and blend until they become a smooth paste, adding a few teaspoons of the filtered water if necessary, about 1 minute. Add the coconut butter, lemon juice, vanilla, and salt. Blend until smooth, scraping down the side of the bowl as needed, about 30 seconds. Add the blueberries and blend, pausing to scrape down the side of the bowl, until incorporated, about 1 minute. Add the almond flour and blend until incorporated, about 20 seconds.

3. Scoop half of the dough into a bowl and set it aside. Scoop out and press the remaining dough into the prepared pan using dampened hands or the back of a spoon. Leave the surface of the dough uneven to create mountainous peaks and valleys. Transfer the dough to the freezer to set while you assemble the cream.

4. Make the cream: Wash and dry the bowl of the food processor. Combine the cashews, coconut milk, honey, lemon juice, and salt in the bowl and blend until smooth, about 30 seconds. Add the coconut butter and coconut flour and blend until smooth, about 15 seconds. Divide the cream among three small bowls. Stir the Blue Majik into one bowl, stir the pitaya powder into the second bowl, and stir the beet powder into the third bowl.

5. Remove the chilled dough from the freezer. Using a spoon, drop the Blue Majik cream, 1 to 2 tablespoons at a time, randomly over the cake, leaving about one third of the Blue Majik cream remaining in the bowl. Sprinkle half of the bee pollen atop. Dollop on the pitaya cream and then the beet cream in the same fashion, reserving one third of each in its respective bowl. Sprinkle the remaining bee pollen atop the cake. Transfer the layer cake to the freezer and freeze until set, about 30 minutes.

6. Remove the cake from the freezer and spread the reserved blueberry dough atop. Return to the freezer for 30 minutes. Remove the cake again and decorate the top with the remaining creams, dropping them by the tablespoonful in any pattern you like. Return to the freezer and freeze until solid, about 4 hours.

7. When ready to serve, remove the cake from the freezer and let it thaw slightly, about 10 minutes. Using a small knife, carefully cut around the sides of the pan to loosen the cake. Then, carefully slide a spatula around and under the bottom of the cake and invert it onto a cutting board. Using a sharp knife, cut the cake crosswise into ¼-inch-thick slices. Serve immediately, sprinkle with extra bee pollen.

Lisa Frank Mountain Cake will keep, wrapped in plastic wrap and then in aluminum foil, in the freezer for about 3 months.

RAW-CACAO-BANANA "ICE CREAM" WITH ALMOND-MACADAMIA CRUMBLE

This banana ice cream is a D R E A M. You can essentially make it from one ingredient alone, and because of banana's pectin content, when you break down the frozen fruit and then whip it, you get a silky smooth and creamy texture. You can really add whatever other ingredients you like, such as almond butter or other types of fruit. I also love to blend in 2 tablespoons of Condensed Coconut Milk (page 168) and ½ teaspoon cinnamon for a refreshing treat! Meanwhile, my boyfriend, Mike, who is a 3-Michelin-star chef, likes to emulsify 3 to 4 tablespoons of melted coconut oil per banana.

While I often top the ice cream with honey and crunchy-sweet almond-macadamia crumble, for a more playful presentation, I scoop it into a gluten-free cone (skipping the honey) and dust it liberally with Natural Rainbow Sprinkles (page 23).

SERVES 4

4 bananas, peeled, frozen, and cut into ½-inch rounds
3 tablespoons raw cacao powder
Pinch of fine sea salt
2 tablespoons raw honey, for serving
Almond-Macadamia Crumble (page 111), for serving

1. Place the frozen banana rounds in a food processor or high-powered blender and process, scraping down the side of the bowl as needed, until the banana has broken down into a creamy, thick, and shiny cream, about 3 minutes. Add the cacao powder and salt and process to blend.

2. Scoop the ice cream into four individual bowls and top each with 1½ teaspoons of the honey and a generous sprinkling of almond-macadamia crumble. Serve immediately.

KIWI-PASSION FRUIT VEGAN CHEESECAKE BARS

Although these pretty green bars are devoid of dairy, you'd have no problem convincing someone otherwise! Using cashews and coconut oil for their creamy base, these delicious chilly sweets are reminiscent of the Italian dessert semifreddo, which is made from frozen cream. To balance out their richness, I've added lime juice and fresh passion fruit for a hit of acidity.

MAKES ABOUT 14 BARS

For the Base
10 pitted dates
6 medium to large dried figs
⅔ cup raw organic almonds
1 tablespoon coconut oil, melted
2 tablespoons unsweetened coconut flakes

For the Filling
3 cups raw/organic cashews, soaked in water to cover overnight, drained
¾ cup coconut oil, melted
¼ cup fresh lime juice
2 passion fruits, halved and pulp scooped out (discard the shells)
2 tablespoons filtered water
½ cup yacon syrup, raw honey, or pure maple syrup
1 vanilla bean, split in half lengthwise and seeds scraped out (reserve the pod for another use)
¼ teaspoon fine sea salt
¼ cup packed fresh baby spinach leaves
4 kiwis, peeled
¼ teaspoon spirulina powder

1. Line a 10 × 7-inch baking pan with parchment paper, extending the paper up and over the sides.

2. Make the base: Combine the dates, figs, almonds, coconut oil, and coconut flakes in a food processor and blend until the mixture is broken down and sticks together, about 1 minute. Transfer the mixture to the prepared pan and, using the back of a spoon, press the mixture firmly into the bottom of the pan.

3. Make the filling: Combine the cashews, coconut oil, lime juice, passion fruit pulp, filtered water, yacon syrup, vanilla seeds, and salt in a blender and process until the mixture is thick and smooth, scraping down the sides as needed, about 30 seconds. Spoon half of the filling into the pan and spread it out with a spoon to coat the base layer. Cover with plastic wrap and transfer to the freezer to set, about 30 minutes.

4. Meanwhile, add the spinach, 2 of the kiwis, and the spirulina to the remaining cashew cream in the blender and process until the spinach leaves are fully broken down and the mixture is light green, about 30 seconds.

5. Remove the baking pan from the freezer, unwrap it, and scoop the kiwi cream atop the cashew cream, using the back of a spoon to smooth the top. Cover the cheesecake again and return it to the freezer until the mixture is set, at least 2 hours.

6. Remove the cheesecake from the freezer and uncover it. Slice the remaining kiwis crosswise into ¼-inch-thick slices and decorate the top of the cheesecake with the fruit by laying the slices side by side. Cover the cheesecake (with a fresh piece of plastic wrap, if needed) and return it to the freezer to set the kiwi slices, 1 hour.

7. Remove the baking pan from the freezer, uncover it, and let the cheesecake defrost to soften slightly, about 10 minutes. Slice the cheesecake into 14 bars and serve.

Kiwi–Passion Fruit Vegan Cheesecake Bars will keep, wrapped well in plastic wrap, and then aluminum foil, in the refrigerator for 1 week, or in the freezer for 1 month.

STRAWBERRY-PINK PEPPERCORN "ICE CREAM" STICKS

M ade from a medley of nuts and fruit, these gluten-free and refined sugar–free "ice cream" sticks will convince you there's life beyond dairy, thanks to a rich cashew cream base. I have a mild obsession with matcha, and therefore thought to add the powdered tea to the base, which serves as both a flavor and color complement to the strawberry. Pink peppercorns add a fun crunch (remember those ice cream cakes with the chocolate crunchies from back in the day?), but if you don't have any, feel free to omit. Note that you'll need to start this recipe a day before you plan to serve it, to give the cashews sufficient time to soak.

MAKES ABOUT 44 SMALL BARS

For the Base
½ cup gluten-free oat flour (see Note)
¼ cup almond flour
¼ cup raw whole almonds
½ cup sliced pitted dates
1 tablespoon filtered water
1 teaspoon pure vanilla extract
1 teaspoon matcha powder
¼ teaspoon fine sea salt

For the Filling
1 cup raw cashews, soaked in tap water to cover overnight
6 tablespoons coconut oil, melted
3 tablespoons fresh lime juice
½ cup raw honey
1 teaspoon pure vanilla extract
¼ teaspoon fine sea salt
1 cup fresh or frozen whole strawberries (about 8 ounces), hulled if fresh
2 tablespoons plus 1½ teaspoons pink peppercorns
Freshly grated zest of 1 orange

1. Make the base: Line an 11 × 7-inch baking pan with parchment paper, extending the paper up and over the sides.

2. Combine the oat flour, almond flour, almonds, dates, filtered water, vanilla extract, matcha powder, and salt in a food processor and process until the mixture is finely ground and begins to stick together and form a dough, about 1 minute. Using your hands or the back of a spoon, press the dough mixture into the prepared pan to form a firmly packed, even layer.

3. Make the filling: Drain the cashews and transfer them to a food processor, along with the coconut oil, lime juice, honey, vanilla extract, and salt. Process until the mixture is smooth and creamy, about 30 seconds. Scoop out half of the cashew mixture and place it in a medium bowl; set it aside.

4. Add ¼ cup of the strawberries (about 2 ounces) to the mixture in the food processor and process until smooth, about 10 seconds. Pour this mixture over the base and use a spatula to smooth it into an even layer. Sprinkle 2 tablespoons of the pink peppercorns atop. Cover with plastic wrap and transfer to the freezer to firm up, about 30 minutes or up to 1 day.

5. Meanwhile, pour the reserved cashew mixture back into the food processor (no need to wipe it out first), add the remaining ¾ cup of strawberries, and the orange zest, and process until smooth and creamy, about 20 seconds.

6. Remove the pan from the freezer and pour the strawberry mixture over the frozen layer, smoothing it into an even layer with a spatula. Sprinkle the remaining 1½ teaspoons of pink peppercorns evenly on top.

7. Cover again and return the "ice cream" to the freezer to set, at least 4 hours and up to 1 day. Remove the ice cream from the freezer and use the parchment paper to lift the whole frozen slab out of the pan. Using a chef's knife, slice the slab into sticks about 3 ½ inches long by ½ inch thick. Serve immediately.

Strawberry–Pink Peppercorn "Ice Cream" Sticks will keep, in an airtight container in the freezer, for up to 3 months.

Note: If you can't find gluten-free oat flour, you can make your own. Simply put 2 cups gluten-free old-fashioned rolled oats in a food processor and blend until pulverized. You may have some leftover; store it in an airtight container at room temperature for up to 6 months.

WASABI FUDGE POPS

Remember when you were a kid and you'd eat those rice pops in narrow plastic tubes? You'd rip off the top and push the pop from the bottom up, nibbling at it until it was done. I'm bringing them back for these spicy fudgy pops, because they're fun to use and easy to find—simply look for the brand Zipzicles online. (If you'd rather use conventional pop molds that come with plastic or wooden sticks, they'll work, too.)

Now, a few notes on this recipe. Depending on how much you like the tingly flavors of fresh ginger and wasabi, you'll want to adjust the quantities to meet your own palate. I tend to like a bit more zing, so if you're less keen on wasabi or ginger, feel free to reduce the amount of either or both.

MAKES SEVEN
9 × 2-INCH POPS

2½ cups coconut milk
2 tablespoons tapioca starch
5 tablespoons raw cacao powder
5 tablespoons coconut palm
 sugar
1½-inch piece (2 ounces) fresh
 ginger, peeled and diced
½ teaspoon pure vanilla extract
Pinch of fine sea salt
4 teaspoons wasabi powder, or
 to taste (see Note)
1 banana, peeled

1. Whisk together ½ cup of the coconut milk and the tapioca starch in a small bowl to make a slurry. Set aside.

2. Heat the remaining 2 cups of coconut milk, the cacao powder, coconut palm sugar, ginger, vanilla, and salt in a medium pot over medium-high heat. When the cacao mixture reaches a boil, whisk in the reserved coconut-tapioca mixture and the wasabi; the mixture will immediately thicken.

3. Remove the mixture from the heat and carefully pour it into a blender. Add the banana and blend until smooth, about 15 seconds.

4. Divide the banana mixture between seven Zipzicle bags and freeze until solid, about 4 hours.

Wasabi Fudge Pops will keep, in the freezer, for up to 4 months.

Note: While fresh wasabi root is rife in Japan, here in the United States it's hard to source the stuff; most of what's available comes either as a powder or a paste. The thing is, many of those products contain flavor boosters like mustard, and artificial colors and other ingredients. So, whatever form you use, make sure to read the label: It should contain only wasabi. I buy pure wasabi powder online from a website called The Spice House.

DIRTY CHAI TAHINI CUPS

With their sweet-savory flavor and creamy richness, these tahini cups are insanely addictive. I keep these guys in the freezer because the mix of frozen coconut oil and tahini paste offers a pleasing bite, which contrasts with the softer date center, flavored with coffee and warming chai spices. It's also that sweet date-based center that balances the savory sesame flavor in the tahini shell.

Note: This dessert is very indulgent! I like to take one cup and cut it into 4 or even 8 slices and serve them, still frozen, at the end of a meal for a sweet finish.

MAKES 9 TAHINI CUPS

⅔ cup tahini (sesame paste)

⅔ cup coconut oil, melted

½ cup pitted dates (about 8 whole dates)

1 teaspoon pure vanilla extract

Scant ½ teaspoon ground cardamom

¼ teaspoon ground cinnamon

⅛ teaspoon fine sea salt

¼ cup strong hot brewed coffee

1. Place the tahini and coconut oil in a medium bowl and whisk to combine. Divide a little bit less than half the mixture among nine silicone cupcake molds, pouring in just enough to cover the bottom of each mold. Transfer the cupcake molds to the freezer to set, about 15 minutes. Reserve the remaining tahini mixture.

2. Meanwhile, place the dates, vanilla extract, cardamom, cinnamon, and salt in a food processor. Add 1 tablespoon of the coffee and blend for about 10 seconds, then scrape down the side of the bowl. Repeat, adding coffee by the tablespoon, until all the coffee is incorporated and the mixture forms a smooth, thick paste.

3. Remove the cupcake molds from the freezer and add 1 teaspoon of the date paste to the center of each, using your fingers or the back of a spoon to press the mixture into a thin layer atop the frozen tahini layer. Divide the reserved tahini mixture among the cups, pouring it on top of the date paste to cover. Return the cupcake molds to the freezer to set, about 20 minutes. Store in the freezer until ready to eat.

4 When ready to serve, remove the cup(s) to a plate and slice into bite-size pieces with a paring knife. Enjoy cold!

Dirty Chai Tahini Cups will keep, in an airtight container in the freezer, for up to 6 months.

Make It Magical

For an extra vitamin and immunity boost, add 1 tablespoon medicinal mushrooms, such as reishi and/or cordyceps, and/or 1 tablespoon tocos when you add the spices in Step 2.

Five

SLATHERS, SPREADS+ SIDEKICKS

Strawberry–Vanilla Bean Chia Jam

Pineapple, Clove, and Black Pepper Jam

Black Honey Tahini

Matcha Honey Butter

Spiced Pumpkin Butter

Not-ella

Tomatillo Salsa

Nori Vinaigrette

Kimchi Dressing

Condensed Coconut Milk

Coconut Whip

Avocado-Grapefruit "Hollandaise"

Tutti-Frutti Dust

Dukkah

Seeded Togarashi

Pastrami Spice

Don't underestimate the power of condiments. From hot sauce to jam, condiments have the ability to quickly elevate basic dishes.

Some of the recipes in the previous chapters rely on condiments and spice blends for an extra boost of flavor and texture, and many of these can be quickly assembled, and stay fresh for an extended period of time. Some of my favorite super-versatile recipes include the Pastrami Spice blend (page 173), which is delicious atop avocado toast or sprinkled on roasted veggies, and the Condensed Coconut Milk (page 168), which works as a dairy replacement in coffee, can be slathered atop Medicine Bread (page 125), and also forms the base for my dairy-free Not-ella (page 163). Then there's my protein-packed Pineapple, Clove, and Black Pepper Jam (page 159), which binds thanks to the addition of chia seeds and works beautifully atop muffins or mixed into overnight oats (see page 57).

Like all condiments, the recipes in this chapter are multipurpose components that easily amplify—or modify—a dish's flavor. You should feel free to get creative and use them in any way that appeals to you. Want to turn your banana smoothie into a berry number? Just stir in some Strawberry–Vanilla Bean Chia Jam (page 158)!

Power Trio (clockwise from bottom):
Pineapple, Clove, and Black Pepper
Jam (page 159), Strawberry–Vanilla
Bean Chia Jam (page 158), and
Medicine Bread (page 125)

STRAWBERRY-VANILLA BEAN CHIA JAM

I've made this jam in various iterations for years. Sometimes I use it atop a biscuit in strawberry shortcake, and sometimes I use these base flavors in a strawberry pie. More recently, I've started to thicken the jam with chia seeds, then keep it in my fridge to put on puddings and cereal and toast. It's delicious as breakfast, dessert, or an afternoon snack sandwiched with almond butter.

The idea here is to cook some of the strawberries to concentrate their flavor, and to add fresh strawberries for texture and acid. While this recipe calls for lemon juice, I've used lime juice and orange juice to great effect. This is one of those recipes that's better the next day, after flavors have time to settle and meld. While you can eat it right away, I suggest prepping it a day ahead.

MAKES ABOUT ⅔ CUP

2 cups large strawberries (preferably organic), hulled and cut into 6 pieces each
2 teaspoons raw honey
1 teaspoon fresh lemon juice
½ vanilla bean, seeds scraped out and pod reserved
Pinch of fine sea salt
1 tablespoon chia seeds

1. Heat 1 cup of the strawberries and the honey in a medium pot over medium heat. Cook, stirring frequently, until the strawberries begin to release their juice and look shiny, about 2 minutes. Add the lemon juice and cook until the strawberries are slightly softened, 2 minutes more. Add another ½ cup of the strawberries and stir to combine.

2. Add the vanilla seeds to the strawberry mixture, then toss in the pod. Reduce the heat to medium-low and cook, stirring frequently, until the strawberries look soft and syrupy, about 4 minutes.

3. Stir in the remaining ½ cup of strawberries, plus the salt and chia seeds. Remove from the heat and let cool. If the

jam is too clumpy, remove the vanilla bean pod (but do not discard it), transfer the jam to a blender, and blend it to break down the berries further, 10 seconds (it will still have some lumps). Transfer the jam and the vanilla bean pod to a glass jar with a lid and chill.

Strawberry–Vanilla Bean Chia Jam will keep, in an airtight container in the refrigerator, for about 1 week.

PINEAPPLE, CLOVE, AND BLACK PEPPER JAM

Sweet and tropical with a savory edge—try spooning this jam atop chia pudding, or even adding it to a smoothie.

1. Place the pineapple chunks in a blender and process until smooth.

2. Pour 2 cups of the pineapple puree (reserve any leftovers for another use) into a medium skillet and add the filtered water, honey, vanilla seeds and pod, cloves, salt, and pepper. Bring to a simmer over medium-low heat, stirring occasionally, until the jam thickens and reduces by half, about 30 minutes.

3. Stir in the orange and lemon juices. Let cool. Transfer the jam to a glass jar with a lid and chill in the refrigerator.

Pineapple, Clove, and Black Pepper Jam will keep, in an airtight container in the refrigerator, for 1 week.

MAKES 1¼ CUPS

½ fresh pineapple, peeled (remove any eyes), cored, and cut into 1-inch chunks
½ cup filtered water
3 tablespoons raw honey
½ vanilla bean, seeds scraped out and pod reserved
⅛ teaspoon ground cloves
⅛ teaspoon fine sea salt
Pinch of freshly ground black pepper
1 tablespoon fresh orange juice
½ teaspoon fresh lemon juice

BLACK HONEY TAHINI

Thanks to the addition of oils, this Middle Eastern-inspired tahini—which takes its unusual hue from black sesame seeds—is a bit lighter than the thick paste you find in jars. It's easier to drizzle atop bananas or baked sweet potatoes (see page 122), and is straight-up delicious.

MAKES ⅓ CUP

¼ cup plus 2 tablespoons black
    sesame seeds, toasted
    (see opposite page)
3 tablespoons canola oil
1 tablespoon toasted sesame oil
1½ teaspoons raw honey
⅛ teaspoon fine sea salt

1. Place the black sesame seeds in a food processor and blend until the seeds begin to break down, about 45 seconds.

2. Add the oils and blend, scraping down side of the bowl with a rubber spatula as needed, until a smooth paste forms, about 3 minutes.

3. Add the honey and salt and blend again to combine.

Black Honey Tahini will keep, in an airtight container in the refrigerator, for about 3 months.

Toasting Seeds and Nuts

Toasting raw nuts and seeds deepens their flavor and gives them a toothsome crunch. There are a few simple ways to do it. No matter which method you use, the toasting will happen quickly, in a matter of minutes depending on the size of the nut or seed, so keep a close eye on them to make sure they don't burn!

On the stovetop: Place the seeds or nuts in a dry frying pan over medium-low heat and cook, stirring frequently, until the seeds or nuts are fragrant and starting to brown (or darken in the case of black sesame seeds). Remove from the heat and let cool completely.

In the oven or toaster oven: Spread the nuts or seeds in a single layer on a parchment paper—or aluminum foil–lined baking sheet and toast at 350°F until fragrant and darker in color.

MATCHA HONEY BUTTER

Sweet and savory with a hint of salt, this matcha butter is awesome in so many ways. Add a dollop atop pancakes or waffles, swipe it across Medicine Bread (page 125), or drop a bit into your a.m. smoothie.

MAKES ½ CUP

½ cup coconut butter

2 teaspoons raw honey

1 teaspoon matcha powder (the highest quality you can find, see page 14)

½ teaspoon fine sea salt

Stir together all of the ingredients in a small bowl until they are thoroughly combined and the mixture is bright green.

Matcha Honey Butter will keep, in an airtight container in the refrigerator, for about 3 months. Bring it to room temperature before serving.

Make It Magical
Add ½ teaspoon of spirulina.

SPICED PUMPKIN BUTTER

've developed a habit of adding about a half teaspoon of coconut oil to my morning coffee when I am out of nut milk—it adds a richness and serves to balance a cup's acidic nature. When I first made this recipe, it was autumn, and one morning when I realized I was out of almond milk and was reaching for the coconut oil, I noticed a jar of this butter I had just made. One scoop later and I felt like I was drinking a healthier version of those horrifically sweet, chemical-laced beverages the coffee chains shill. This pumpkin butter—delicious in a drink or smeared atop a muffin or toast—delivers a taste of fall temps via clean ingredients.

MAKES ½ CUP

½ cup canned organic
   pumpkin puree
¼ cup plus 2 tablespoons
   coconut oil
2 tablespoons pure maple syrup
1½ teaspoons ground cinnamon
½ teaspoon ground ginger
½ teaspoon ground nutmeg
½ teaspoon ground allspice
¼ teaspoon ground cloves
⅛ teaspoon fine sea salt, plus
   extra as needed
Pinch of freshly ground
   black pepper

1. Combine all of the ingredients in a medium pot over medium heat and cook, whisking occasionally, until incorporated, about 5 minutes.

2. If the oil and pumpkin have not combined, while the mixture is still warm, transfer it to a blender and blend until fully emulsified, about 30 seconds. Let cool before using.

Spiced Pumpkin Butter will keep, in an airtight container in the refrigerator, for about 1 week. Bring to room temperature before serving.

NOT-ELLA

Like so many people, I am a huge fan of Nutella, the beloved spread made from chocolate and hazelnuts. But I'm less a fan of some of the spread's ingredients—namely dairy and tons of sugar! This recipe sidesteps milk with coconut as the base, yielding a less sweet spread that's shockingly similar to the original.

If you read the headnote to the Condensed Coconut Milk recipe (on page 168), you'll see I talk about the differences between coconut milk made with and without stabilizers. If you make the condensed milk recipe with a coconut milk containing a stabilizer, just be aware that it will take on a slightly firm, fudgelike quality; using coconut milk without a stabilizer will yield a softer spread.

MAKES 1½ CUPS

2 cups raw hazelnuts, preferably organic
1 recipe Condensed Coconut Milk (page 168)
5 tablespoons raw cacao powder
2 teaspoons pure vanilla extract
¾ teaspoon fine sea salt

1. Preheat the oven to 350°F.

2. Place the hazelnuts on a rimmed baking sheet and toast until light brown and fragrant and the skins begin to split, about 10 minutes. While the nuts are still hot, wrap them loosely in a clean kitchen towel and rub them together in the towel to remove the skins. Let cool.

3. Place the toasted, skinned hazelnuts in a food processor and blend, pausing occasionally to scrape down the side of the bowl with a rubber spatula, until the nuts turn into a paste and become oily, about 5 minutes.

4. Add the condensed coconut milk, cacao powder, vanilla, and salt and blend until thick and smooth.

Not-ella will keep, in an airtight container in the refrigerator, for up to 2 weeks.

TOMATILLO SALSA

I love the flavor, acidity, and slickness of tomatillo salsa. It is great on avocado pizza (see page 102), and it's also a perfect friend to tortilla chips (*natch*). You can also serve it atop steamed vegetables, or even as a salad dressing.

(see page 102)

1. Preheat the oven to broil.

2. Place the tomatillos and serrano on a rimmed baking sheet and broil until the tomatillos start to speckle with brown spots, about 7 minutes. Remove the baking sheet from the oven and, using a spatula, flip the tomatillos and serrano over. Return to the oven and broil until brown spots form on the opposite side, about 7 minutes.

3. Transfer the tomatillos to a food processor and the serrano to a cutting board. Let the serrano cool to the touch. Cut off and discard the stem of the serrano and add the chile to the food processor, along with the cilantro, onion, lime juice, garlic, the ½ teaspoon of salt, and the jalapeño. Process until the salsa takes on a texture a bit thicker than hot sauce, about 1 minute. Season to taste with salt.

Tomatillo Salsa will keep, in an airtight container in the refrigerator, for about 4 days.

MAKES ABOUT 1 CUP

4 medium tomatillos, husks removed, fruits washed to remove sticky residue

1 fresh serrano chile (about 3 inches long)

2 tablespoons coarsely chopped fresh cilantro

2 tablespoons chopped white onion

2 tablespoons fresh lime juice

2 garlic cloves, peeled

½ teaspoon fine sea salt, plus extra as needed

¼-inch-thick slice jalapeño (seeds removed for less heat if desired)

NORI VINAIGRETTE

This spicy seaweed dressing gets its kick from fresh garlic, ginger, and a bit of rice wine vinegar. The nori adds a savory umami flavor, while orange and honey offer balance. Try this as a salad dressing, or even as a dip for crudités.

MAKES ABOUT 1 CUP

3 tablespoons rice wine vinegar
3 tablespoons fresh orange juice
2 garlic cloves, peeled
1½ sheets nori, toasted
½ large shallot, peeled
⅓ ounce fresh ginger, peeled
1½ teaspoons raw honey
½ teaspoon fine sea salt
½ cup vegetable oil
About 2 tablespoons filtered water

1. Combine the vinegar, orange juice, garlic, nori, shallot, ginger, honey, and salt in a food processor and blend to incorporate, pausing to scrape down the side of the bowl as needed, about 2 minutes.

2. With the motor running, slowly add the oil in increments to emulsify. Blend in the filtered water, beginning with 2 tablespoons and adding a bit more if desired, to lighten the vinaigrette.

Nori Vinaigrette will keep, in an airtight container in the refrigerator, for about 3 days.

KIMCHI DRESSING

Hot and fermented, this super-versatile chile sauce—which is equal parts hot sauce and dressing—uses kimchi as its base flavor. Additional heat and fermented notes come from a Korean condiment called gochujang, which is made from chiles, glutinous rice (which, for the record, is gluten-free!), fermented soybeans, and salt—it's sort of like a spicy take on miso paste. This kimchi sauce is salty, sour, and sweet, and offers a huge burst of flavor that enhances raw or roasted veggies. Add it to a salad for a touch of heat, or dash it atop avocado toast.

MAKES ABOUT ⅔ CUP
¼ cup kimchi juice
   (from a jar of kimchi)
¼ cup gluten-free soy sauce
¼ cup gochujang (see Note)
4 teaspoons coconut palm sugar
2 tablespoons rice vinegar
2 tablespoons canola oil
1 teaspoon fresh lime juice

Combine all of the ingredients in a blender and puree until they are fully incorporated and the sauce has a thick but pourable texture, about 20 seconds.

Kimchi Dressing will keep, in an airtight container in the refrigerator, for about 3 days.

Note: Gochujang is sold at some supermarkets and Asian markets, and is widely available online.

CONDENSED COCONUT MILK

Traditional condensed milk is a canned product that's for sale at most markets, and it's made from cow's milk that has been cooked down to a thick, syrupy consistency and spiked with sugar. It makes delicious—if sweet—coffee drinks, and it's the dairy component in Thai iced tea. It's also used as a topping for some Asian desserts. As a fan of the product, I set out to create a less-sweet, dairy-free option based on canned coconut milk.

It's important to note that not all canned coconut milk is made with the same ingredients. There's more on this in Chapter 1 (see pages 8–9), but I look for brands that don't have any added stabilizers like guar gum, which is often an extra ingredient alongside coconut and sometimes water. You can make this recipe with either type of canned coconut milk: with or without added stabilizers. If you use one containing a stabilizer, the condensed milk will take on a slightly more gel-like texture; an additive-free coconut milk will yield a condensed milk that's more pastelike. The latter version also separates a bit when cooked—you can either mix the separated oil back in, or refrigerate the condensed coconut milk until the oil solidifies at the top and you can easily remove it.

MAKES 1 CUP

2 cups coconut milk
1 cup coconut palm sugar
⅛ teaspoon fine sea salt

Combine all of the ingredients in a medium pot over medium-low heat and simmer, stirring frequently, until the mixture is syrupy and reduced by half, about 45 minutes.

Remove from the heat and let cool.

Condensed Coconut Milk will keep, in an airtight container in the refrigerator, for 2 weeks.

COCONUT WHIP

Think of this multipurpose coconut whip as you would whipped cream, though one made from a plant-based source. Use it anywhere you'd use traditional whipped cream—atop beverages, on ice cream, and spooned over desserts for an extra creamy touch. As I mentioned on page 168, coconut milk without stabilizers separates better—for this recipe, look for the 100% pure stuff.

MAKES ABOUT ¾ CUP

1 can (14 ounces) full-fat coconut milk, refrigerated unopened and unshaken overnight
1 teaspoon pure vanilla extract
1 teaspoon coconut palm sugar
Pinch of salt (I like pink Himalayan salt)

Open the can of coconut milk; the thick coconut cream sits at the top and the coconut water below it. Using a spoon, scoop out the cream and transfer it to the bowl of a stand mixer fitted with the whisk attachment (or into a large bowl, if using an electric hand mixer); reserve the coconut water for another use. Add the vanilla, coconut palm sugar, and salt, and whisk together on high speed until the mixture resembles whipped cream, about 1 minute. Serve immediately.

AVOCADO-GRAPEFRUIT "HOLLANDAISE"

Think about this sauce as a replacement for mayo. It's thick, creamy—just like mayo—with a hit of citrus and mild bitterness from the grapefruit. You can use it in a veggie or grain bowl, atop proteins, in a sandwich or wrap, or as a dip for crudités.

MAKES ¾ CUP

1 avocado, peeled and pitted
Juice and finely grated zest of
   1 grapefruit
3 tablespoons olive oil
1 tablespoon filtered water
2 teaspoons apple cider vinegar
2 teaspoons raw honey
¼ teaspoon cayenne pepper
½ teaspoon fine sea salt

Combine all of the ingredients in a food processor or blender and process until they are fully incorporated and the sauce is pale green and velvety, about 1 minute. Transfer to a bowl and serve immediately.

TUTTI-FRUTTI DUST

This simple, delicious pixie dust is excellent on waffles (see page 67). And pancakes. And custards (see pages 60–63). And cereal. And smoothie bowls. It makes pretty much everything better.

MAKES 4½ TEASPOONS
¼ cup freeze-dried strawberries
¼ cup freeze-dried bananas

Combine the freeze-dried fruit in a ziplock bag and seal the bag. Roll a wine bottle, jar, or even a rolling pin (!) over the bag to coarsely crush the fruit. The dust should be mostly powder, with some larger chunks.

Tutti-Frutti Dust will keep, in an airtight container at room temperature, for 1 month.

DUKKAH

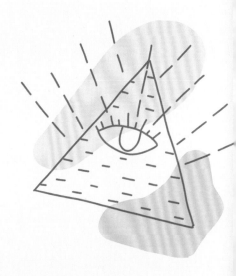

Dukkah is a crunchy Egyptian nut, spice, and (sometimes) herb mixture that's traditionally served as an accompaniment to bread. I've also seen dukkah used as a garnish for yogurt and various proteins, but it's equally delicious atop roasted veggies, or adding a savory spin to morning oatmeal. Try sprinkling it on hummus (and Beet Hummus, page 118), avocado, or even a grain bowl. It's spicy, earthy, and nutty all in one!

1. Preheat the oven to 350°F.

2. Place the hazelnuts on a rimmed baking sheet and toast until light brown and fragrant, about 7 minutes. While the nuts are still hot, wrap them loosely in a clean kitchen towel and rub them together in the towel to remove the skins. Let cool.

3. Place the sesame seeds in a small, dry skillet and toast over medium heat, stirring frequently, until golden, about 4 minutes. Pour the seeds into a medium bowl.

4. Using the same skillet, toast the coriander and cumin seeds over medium heat until they become fragrant, about 1 minute. Remove from the heat and pour the hot seeds into a food processor. Process the seeds until finely ground, about 5 minutes, then add them to the sesame seeds.

5. Place the cooled hazelnuts in the food processor and process until finely ground, about 30 seconds. Add the ground hazelnuts to the sesame seed mixture and stir to blend. Stir in the salt and pepper, taste and add more salt if needed.

Dukkah will keep, in an airtight container at room temperature, for about 1 month.

MAKES ¼ CUP

½ cup raw hazelnuts, preferably organic

4 teaspoons white sesame seeds

1 teaspoon coriander seeds

1 teaspoon cumin seeds

½ teaspoon fine sea salt, plus extra as needed

½ teaspoon freshly ground black pepper

SEEDED TOGARASHI

Togarashi, also known as *shichimi togarashi*, is a common Japanese spice blend made from seven ingredients. While those ingredients and their quantities can vary, the base players are usually sesame seeds (white and/or black), seaweed, dried ginger, chiles, Sichuan peppercorns, poppy seeds, and dried orange peel. Try sprinkling togarashi on roasted veggies, avocado toast, or salad.

MAKES ⅔ CUP

4 garlic cloves, peeled

2 sheets nori, torn into small pieces

2 tablespoons raw, unsalted sunflower seeds

2 teaspoons white or black sesame seeds, or a combination

2 teaspoons freshly grated orange zest

½ teaspoon fine sea salt

½ teaspoon freshly ground black pepper

½ teaspoon crushed red pepper flakes

....

1. Preheat the oven to 350°F.

2. Combine all of the ingredients in a food processor and pulse until broken down and incorporated, about 1 minute. Transfer the mixture to a rimmed baking sheet and bake until the mixture is dry and crispy, about 5 minutes.

Let cool on the baking sheet; as the mixture cools, it will dry out even more.

Seeded Togarashi will keep, in an airtight container at room temperature, for 1 day, or in the refrigerator for 5 days. Retoast it in a 350°F oven for a few minutes before using.

PASTRAMI SPICE

Inspired by the classic spice blend used to coat pastrami beef, this savory mélange of seeds and spices is equally delicious rubbed onto the outside of beets, sprinkled atop other veggies like roasted cauliflower, or added to avocado toast for a burst of flavor. While pastrami spice is often made with paprika, here I've subbed in garam masala, which is itself an Indian spice blend of chile and warm spices such as cinnamon, cardamom, cloves, and nutmeg. The garam masala adds an exotic twist to this traditional American rub.

MAKES ABOUT ⅓ CUP

1 teaspoon mustard seeds
1 teaspoon coriander seeds
1 tablespoon coconut palm sugar
1 tablespoon garlic powder
1 tablespoon onion powder
1 teaspoon garam masala
1 teaspoon freshly ground
    black pepper

....

Using a mortar and pestle or a food processor, blend all of the ingredients together until the spices are coarsely ground and combined (they should not be completely broken down into a fine dust).

Pastrami Spice will keep, in an airtight container at room temperature, for 3 months.

CONVERSION TABLES

P lease note that all conversions are approximate but close enough to be useful when converting from one system to another.

OVEN TEMPERATURES

FAHRENHEIT	GAS MARK	CELSIUS
250	½	120
275	1	140
300	2	150
325	3	160
350	4	180
375	5	190
400	6	200
425	7	220
450	8	230
475	9	240
500	10	260

Note: Reduce the temperature by 20°C (68°F) for fan-assisted ovens.

APPROXIMATE EQUIVALENTS

1 stick butter = 8 tbs = 4 oz = ½ cup = 115 g

1 cup all-purpose presifted flour = 4.7 oz

1 cup granulated sugar = 8 oz = 220 g

1 cup (firmly packed) brown sugar = 6 oz = 220 g to 230 g

1 cup confectioners' sugar = 4½ oz = 115 g

1 cup honey or syrup = 12 oz

1 cup grated cheese = 4 oz

1 cup dried beans = 6 oz

1 large egg = about 2 oz or about 3 tbs

1 egg yolk = about 1 tbs

1 egg white = about 2 tbs

LIQUID CONVERSIONS

U.S.	IMPERIAL	METRIC
2 tbs	1 fl oz	30 ml
3 tbs	1½ fl oz	45 ml
¼ cup	2 fl oz	60 ml
⅓ cup	2½ fl oz	75 ml
⅓ cup + 1 tbs	3 fl oz	90 ml
⅓ cup + 2 tbs	3½ fl oz	100 ml
½ cup	4 fl oz	125 ml
⅔ cup	5 fl oz	150 ml
¾ cup	6 fl oz	175 ml
¾ cup + 2 tbs	7 fl oz	200 ml
1 cup	8 fl oz	250 ml
1 cup + 2 tbs	9 fl oz	275 ml
1¼ cups	10 fl oz	300 ml
1⅓ cups	11 fl oz	325 ml
1½ cups	12 fl oz	350 ml
1² cups	13 fl oz	375 ml
1¾ cups	14 fl oz	400 ml
1¾ cups + 2 tbs	15 fl oz	450 ml
2 cups (1 pint)	16 fl oz	500 ml
2½ cups	20 fl oz (1 pint)	600 ml
3¾ cups	1½ pints	900 ml
4 cups	1¾ pints	1 liter

WEIGHT CONVERSIONS

U.S./U.K.	METRIC	U.S./U.K.	METRIC
½ oz	15 g	7 oz	200 g
1 oz	30 g	8 oz	250 g
1½ oz	45 g	9 oz	275 g
2 oz	60 g	10 oz	300 g
2½ oz	75 g	11 oz	325 g
3 oz	90 g	12 oz	350 g
3½ oz	100 g	13 oz	375 g
4 oz	125 g	14 oz	400 g
5 oz	150 g	15 oz	450 g
6 oz	175 g	1 lb	500 g

INDEX

ACKNOWLEDGMENTS

I'd like to thank my grandmother for being an amazing cook and introducing me to the kitchen at a very young age.

I'd like to thank my parents (and especially my dad) for letting me dump all the saffron in the soup. And Mom, thanks for believing in clean, whole, organic foods before it was a thing. And for growing a garden with five kinds of basil.

Peter and Emmy, thanks for consistency-sampling all of my efforts and taste-testing this book along the way. Oli and Tig too, kinda.

To my boyfriend, Mike, thank you for embracing medicinal, plant-based foods. You're a constant inspiration in my life.

A tremendous thanks to my amazing, forward-thinking editor, Kylie Foxx McDonald, for believing in *Unicorn Food* way back in 2014 before this current rainbow food craze overtook the internet. And thank you for also serving as a guinea pig and taste-testing many of these recipes along the way. Thanks so much for all of your diligent efforts and supporting my very out-there ideas!

Mailea Weger, thank you for all of your time and effort working with me on developing some of the recipes in this book. Thanks for hanging in my tiny NYC kitchen and coloring things pink, purple, and red. ☺

Thank you to everyone else at Workman who helped this book come to be, especially Becky Terhune for her graphic design expertise, Anne Kerman, Kate Karol, Rachael Mt. Pleasant, Barbara Peragine, Chloe Puton, and Moira Kerrigan.

AJ Meeker, you nailed the look with your photography. I am obsessed with how all the images came out. Kaitlyn Du Ross and Rebecca Jurkevich (and Lauren Schaefer!), you entirely understood my vision for this book. Thank you so much for your excellent eye and aesthetic. And to Michelle Mildenberg, too, for her beautiful illustrations. This book would have looked very different without you.

ABOUT THE AUTHOR

KAT ODELL is the entrepreneur behind the plant-based food and drink brand Unicorn Food, as well as a food and travel journalist. She was the inaugural editor of Eater Drinks and was the editor of Eater LA for five years. She has been published in *Vogue*, the *New York Times T Magazine*, *Travel + Leisure*, *Condé Nast Traveler*, and *Bon Appétit*, among others. She has also served as a judge and expert at a variety of food-related events. Kat Odell and Unicorn Food can be found at @kat_odell and @unicornfoods.